CLOSE OUT

Brian Ulrich

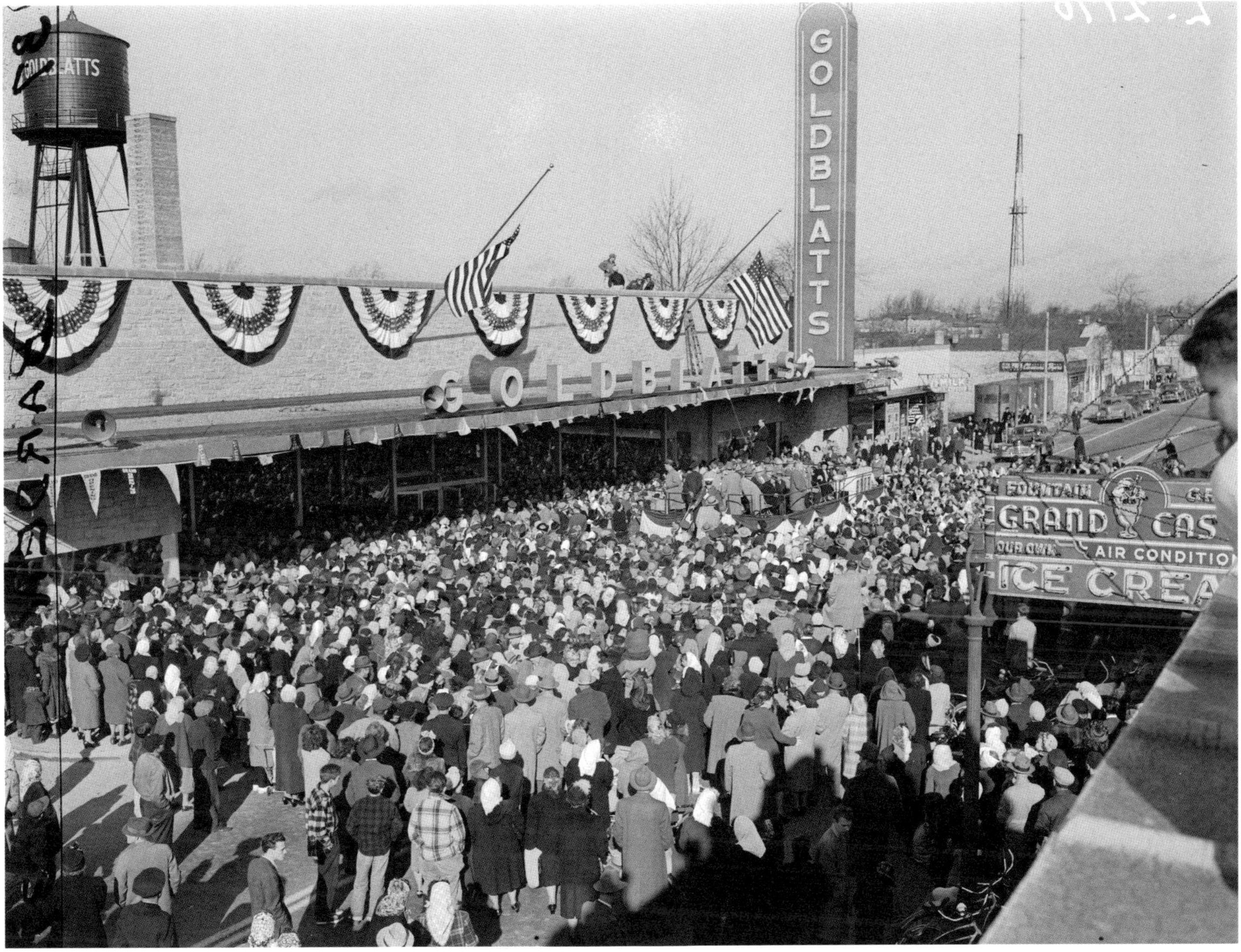

Goldblatt's "Store of the Future," Chicago

1948

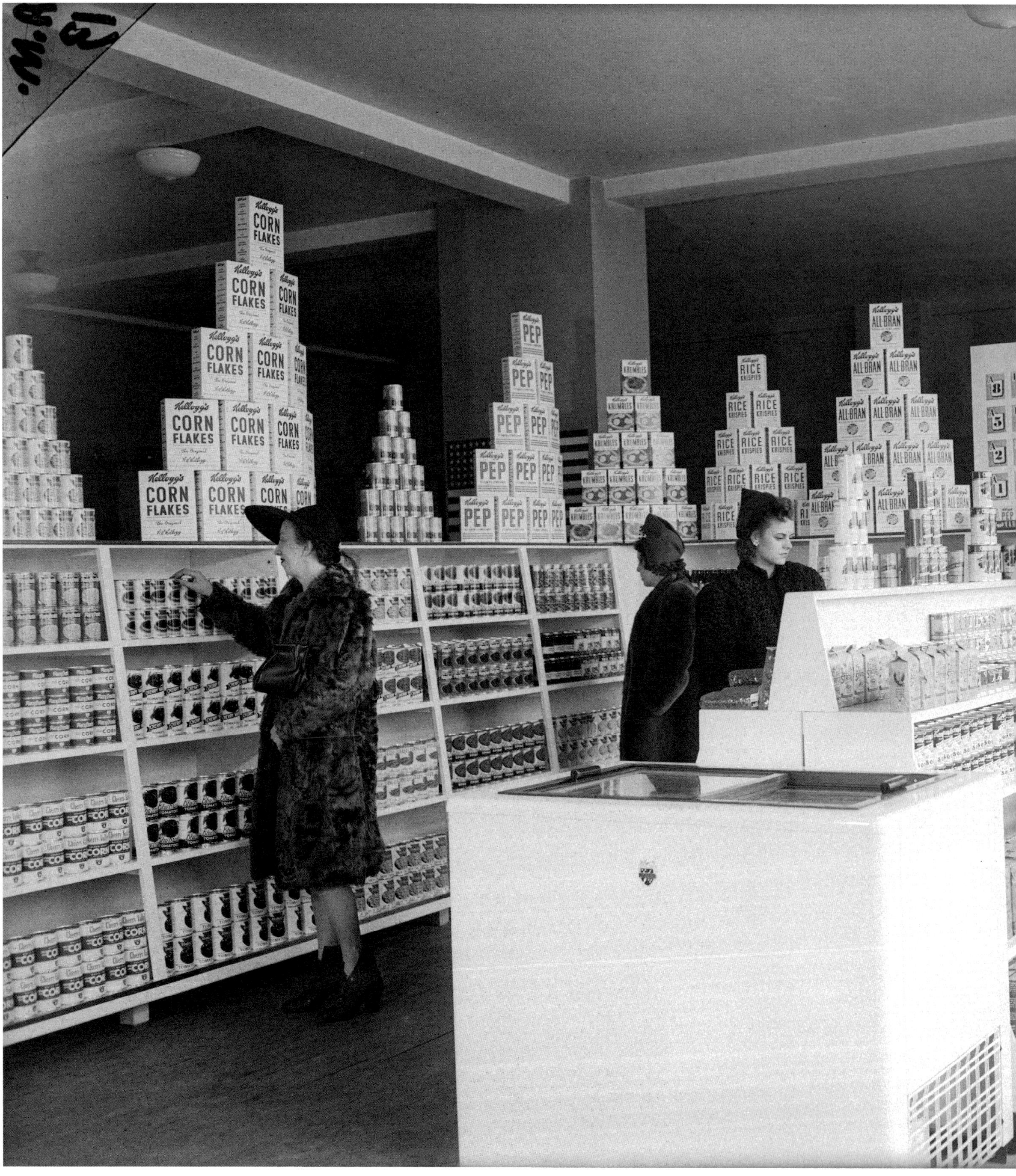

OPA Model Grocery Store, Chicago

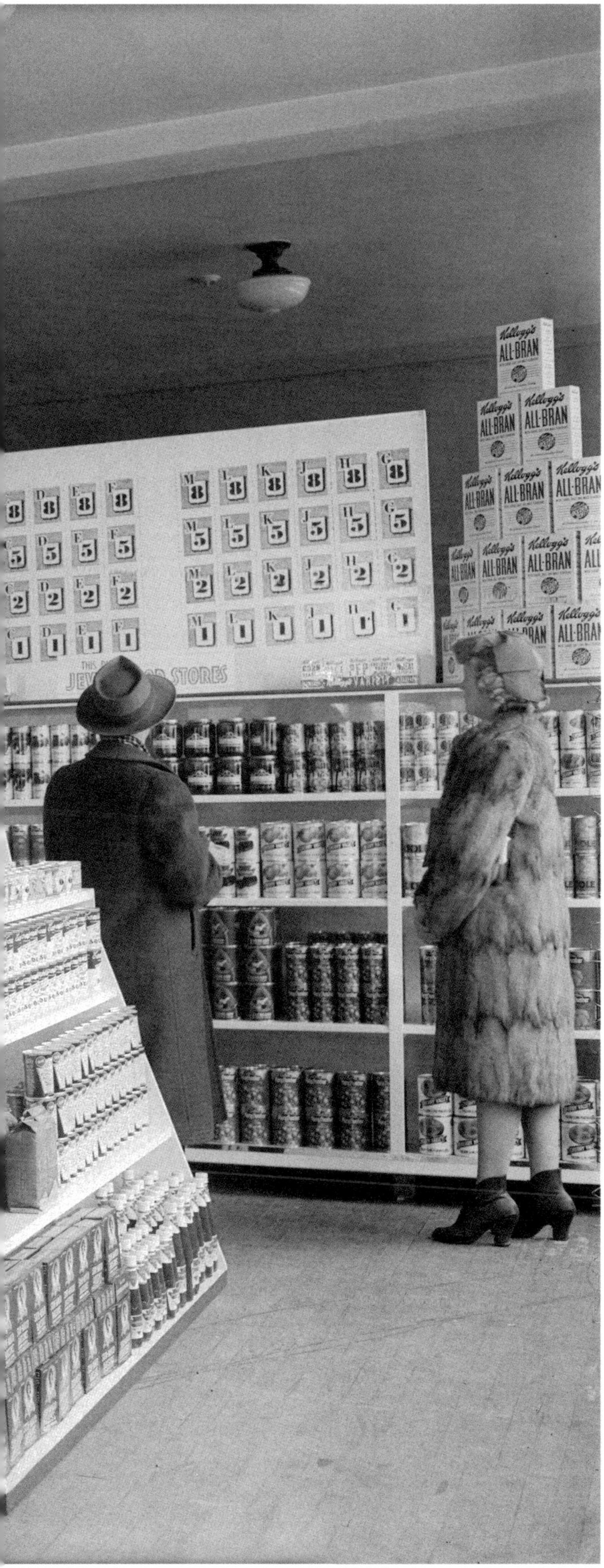

1943

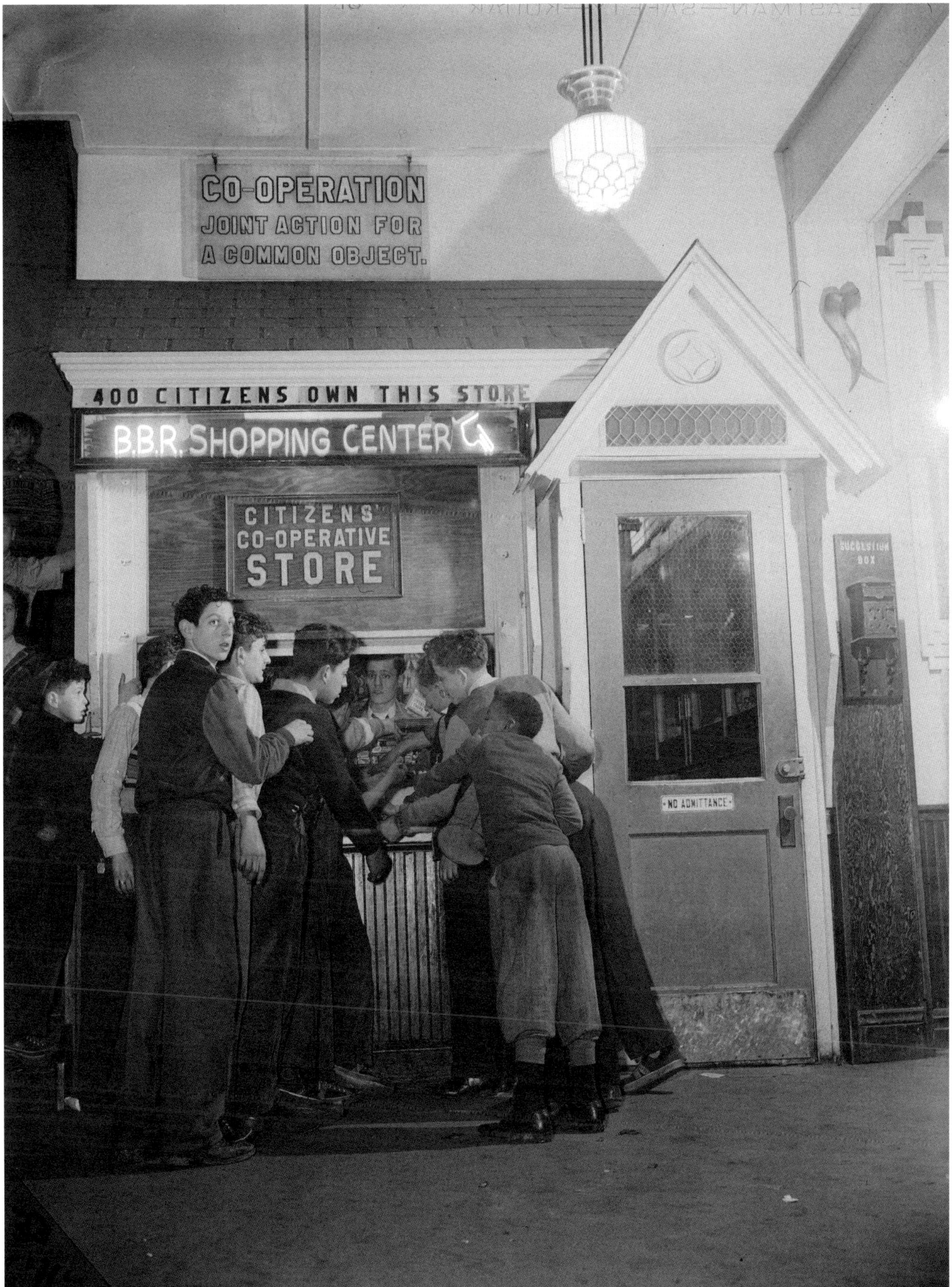

Citizens Cooperative Store, Boys Brotherhood Republic, Chicago 1942

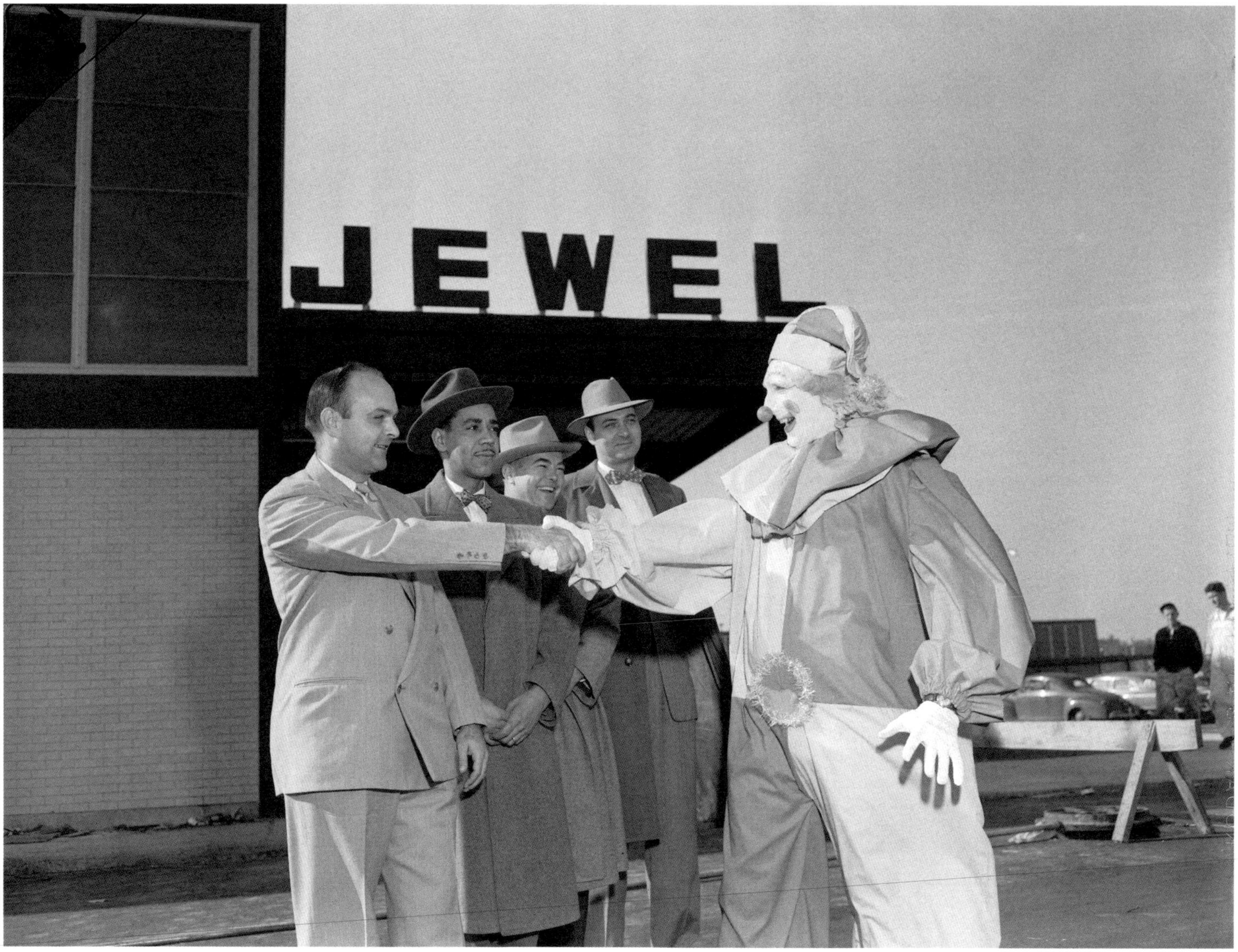

Jewel Food Store, Lake Meadows Center, Chicago 1954

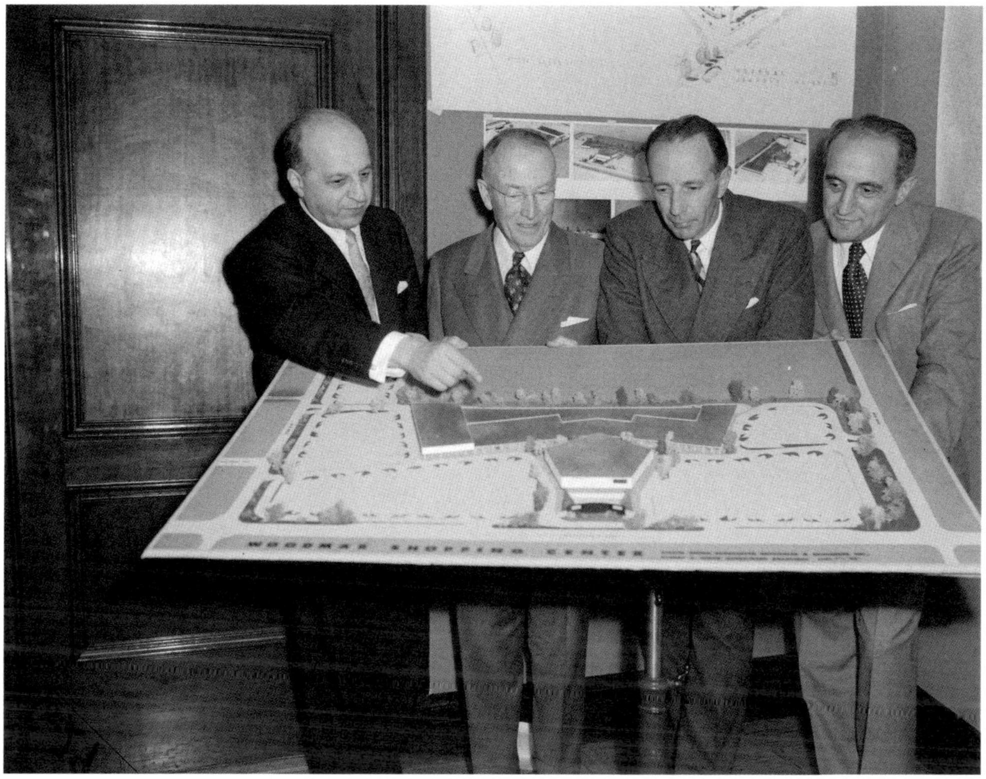

Proposed Shopping Center, Hammond, Indiana 1953

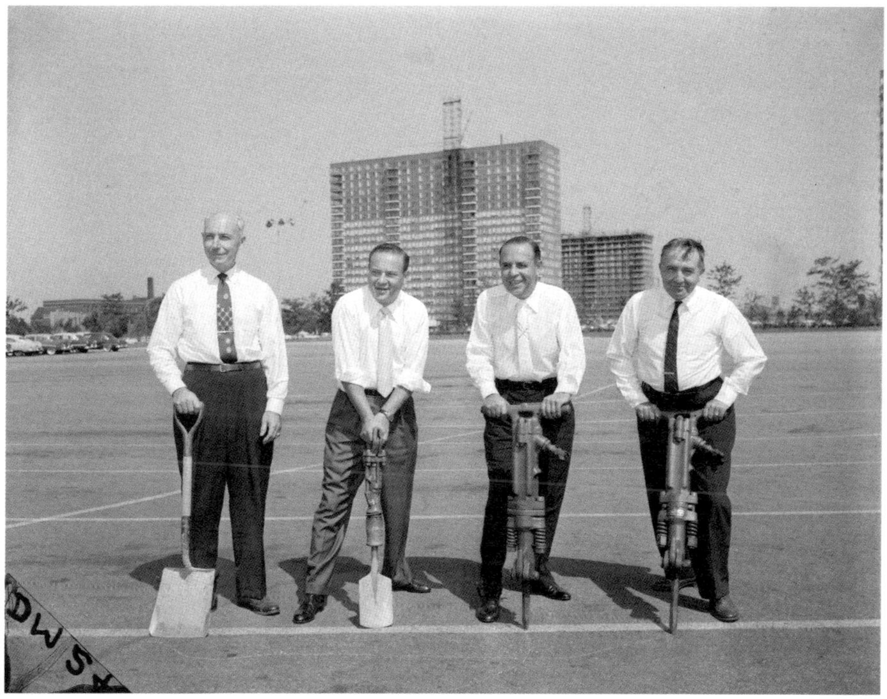

Groundbreaking, New Goldblatt's store, Lake Meadows Center, Chicago 1957

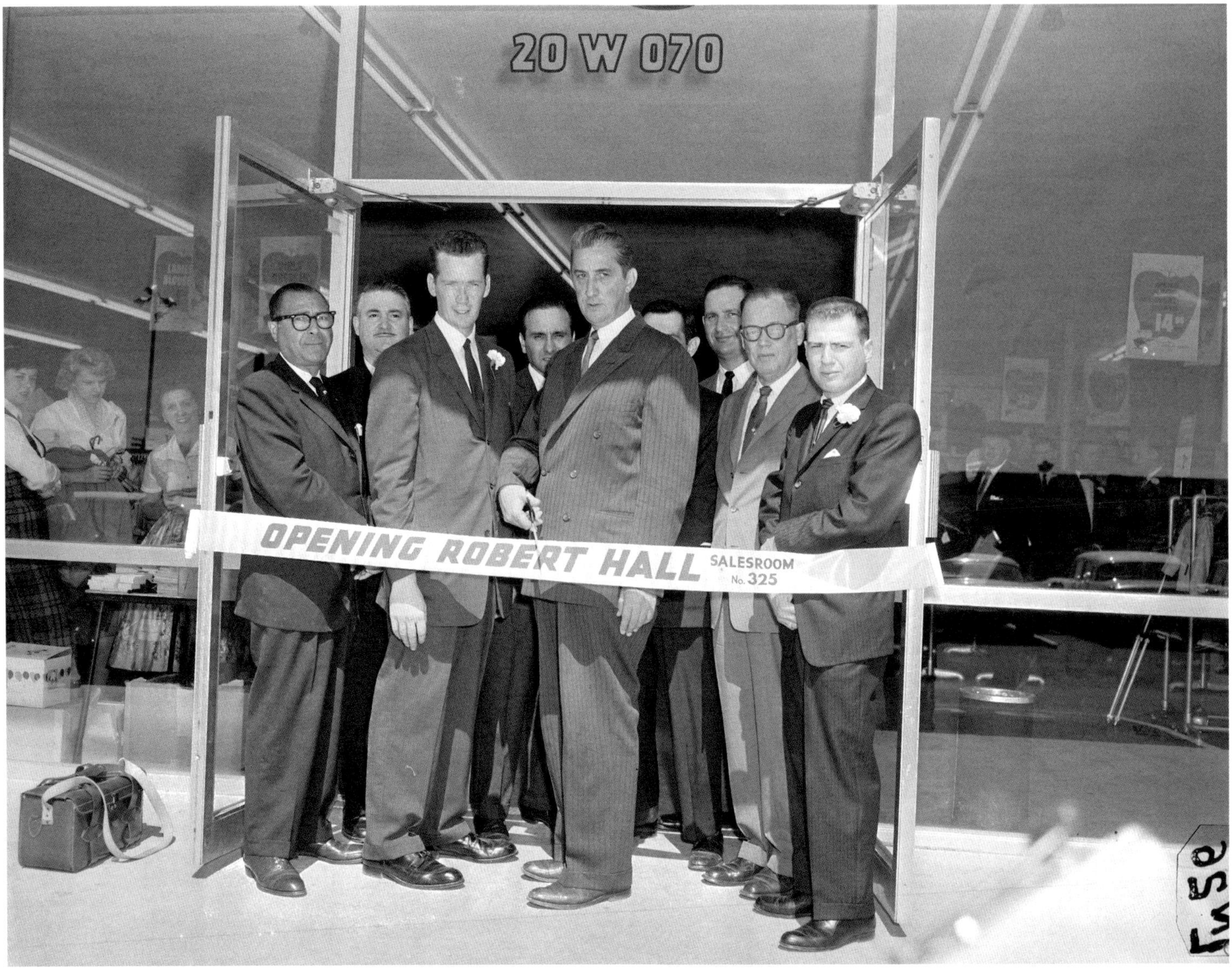

Opening, Robert Hall Store, Downers Grove, Illinois 1959

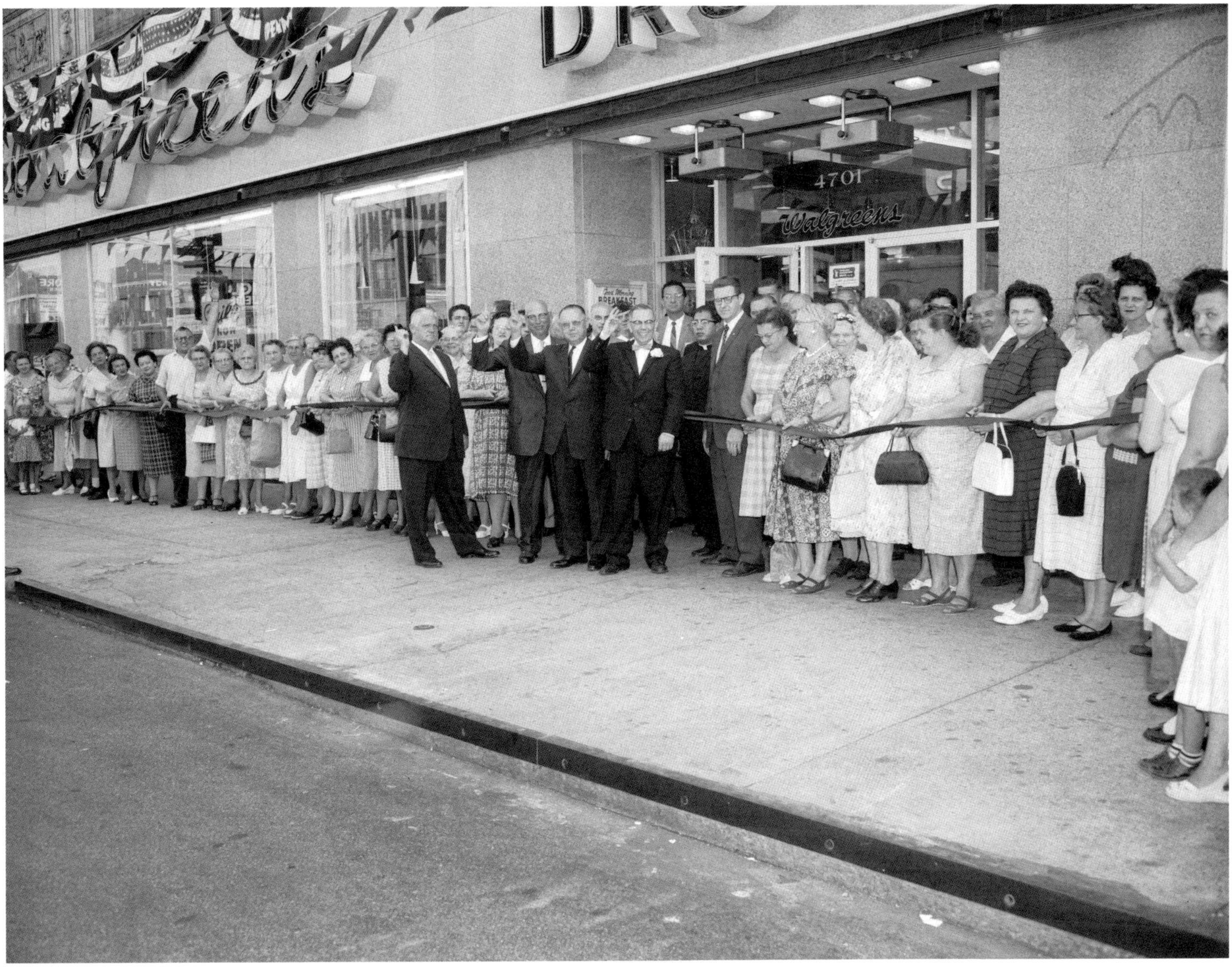

Opening, Walgreens Drug Store, Chicago 1960

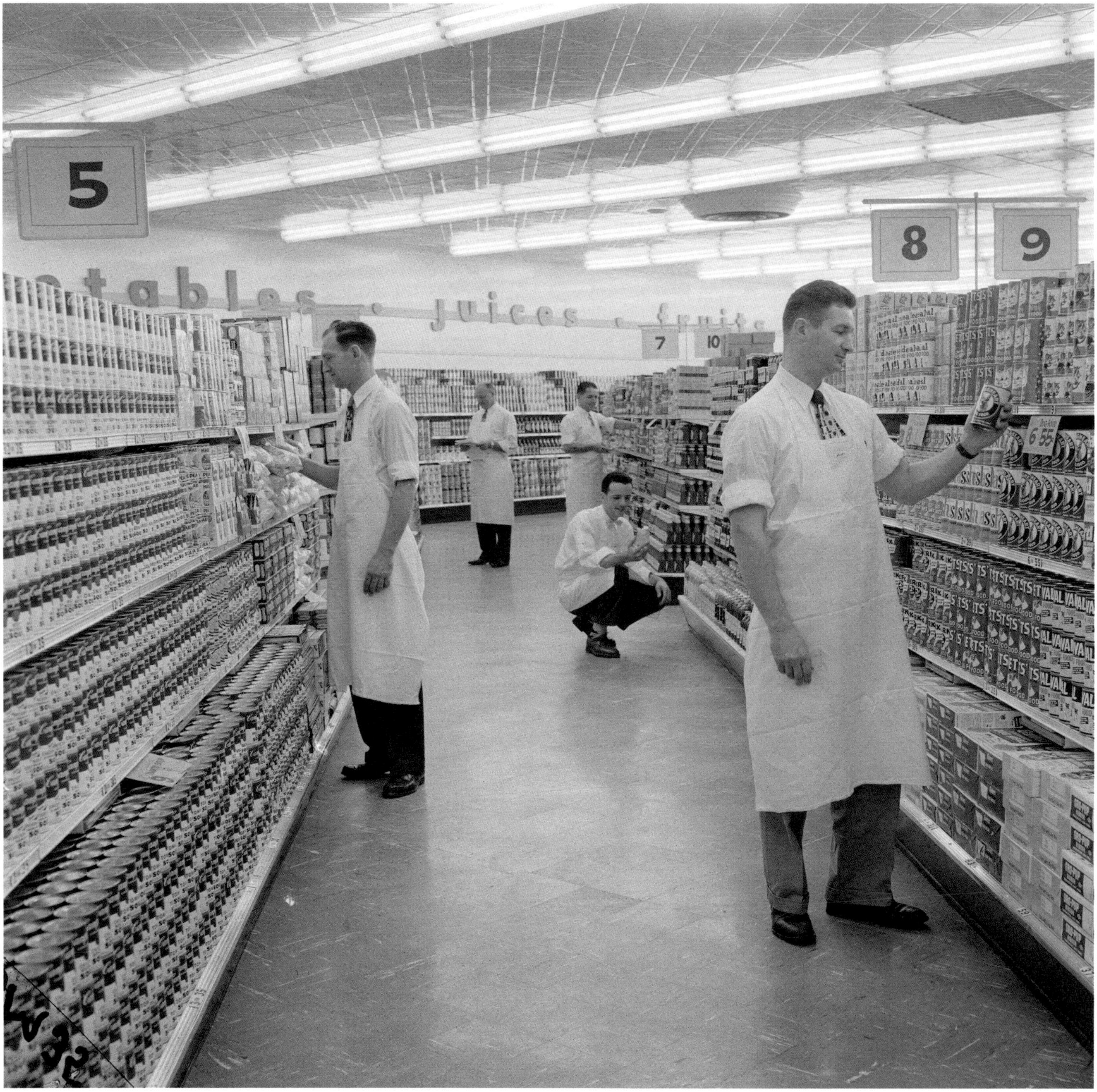

New Jewel Food Store, Lisle, Illinois 1956

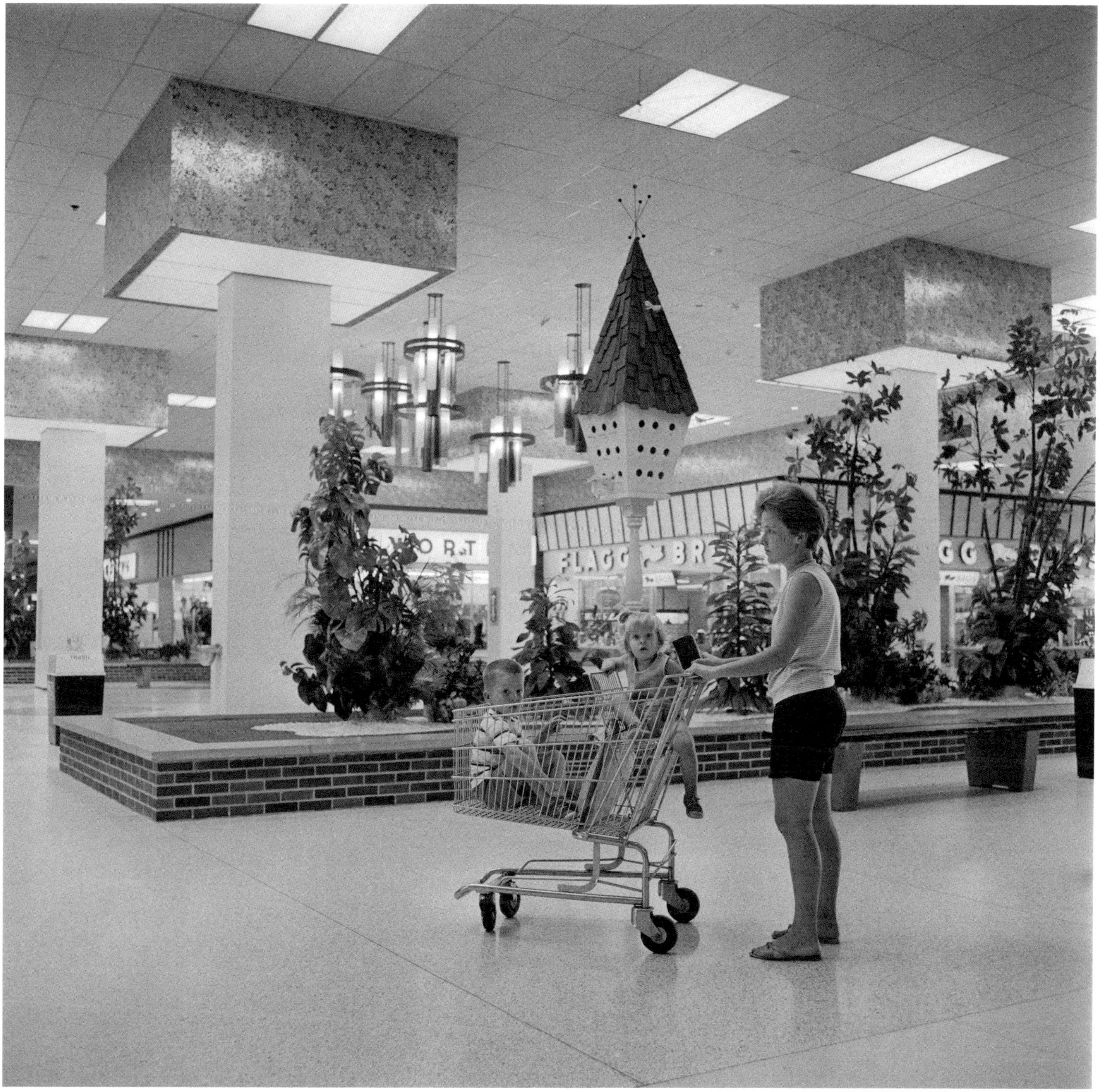

Interior, Ford City Mall, Chicago 1966

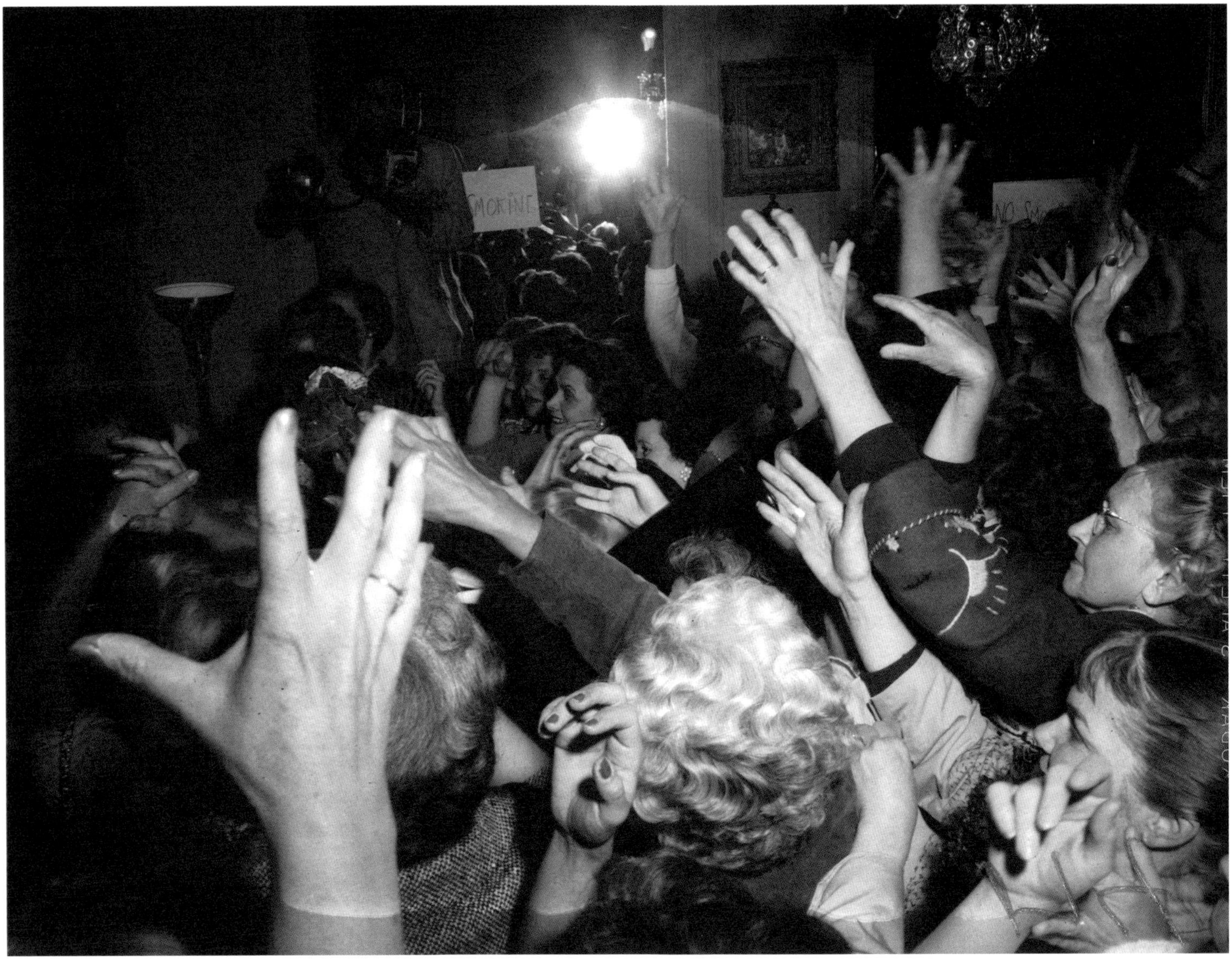

Annual Sale, Bes-Ben Hat Shop, Chicago 1962

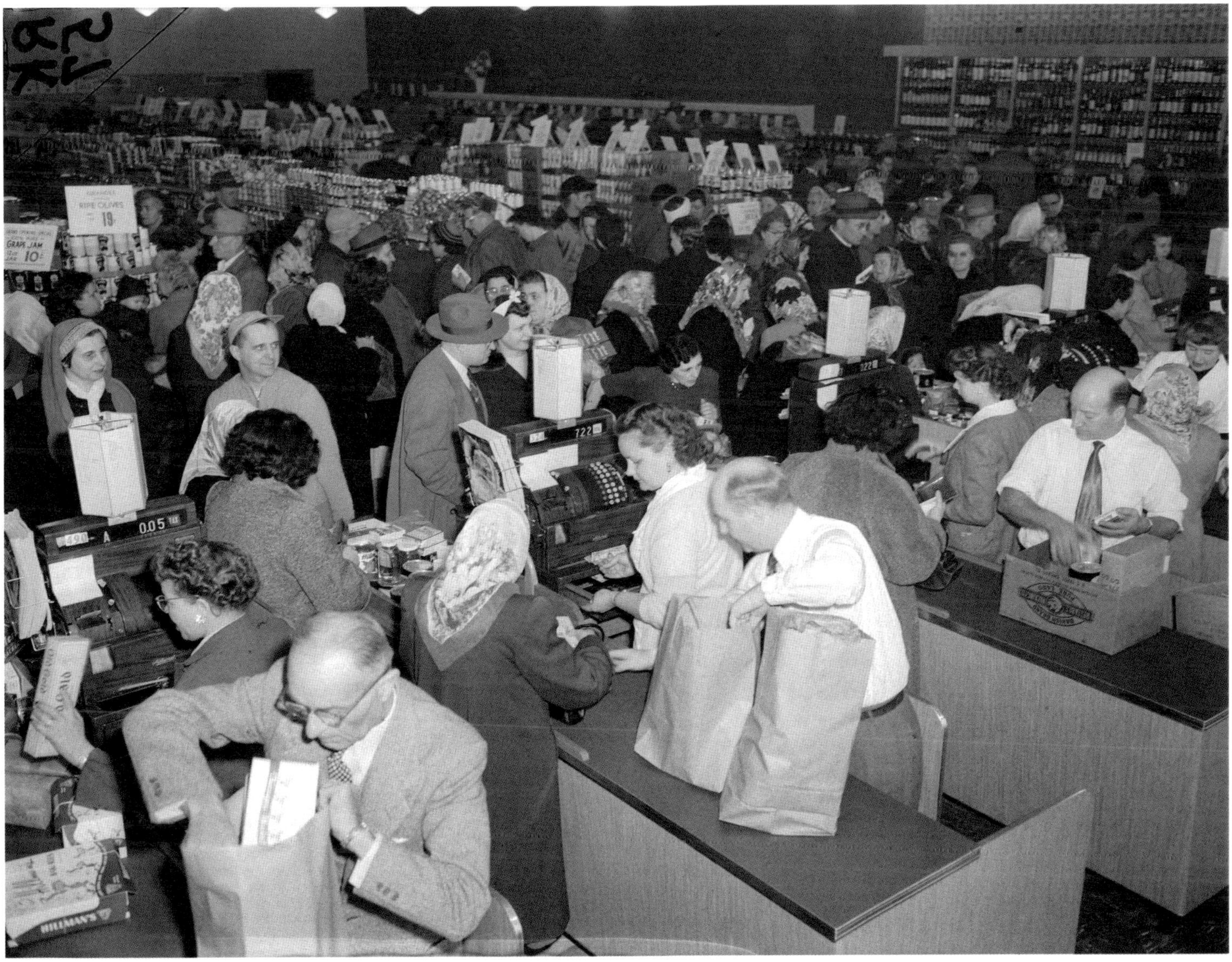

Hillman's New Store n.d.

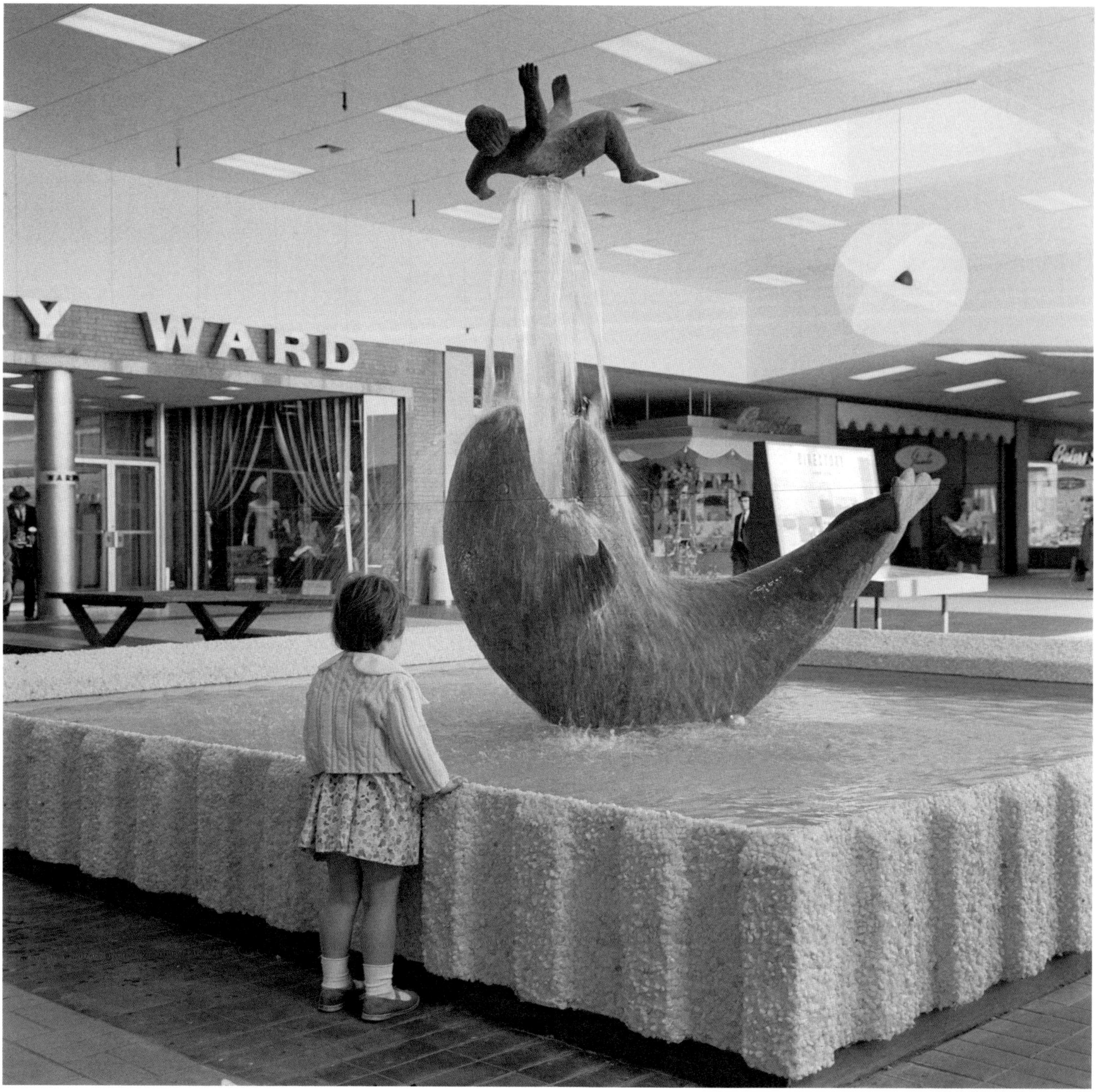

Whale Fountain, Evergreen Plaza Mall, Evergreen Park, Illinois 1966

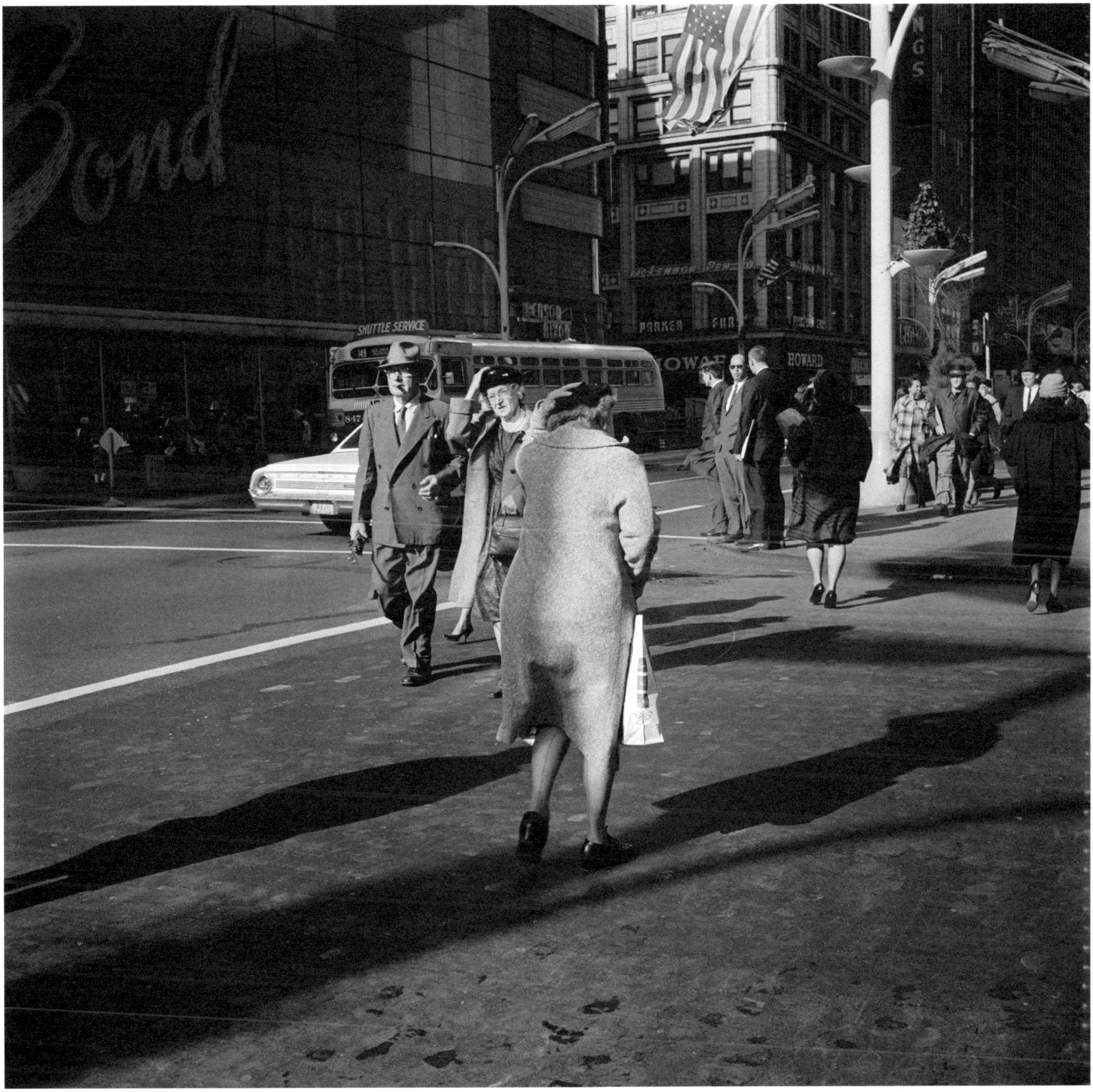

Chicago Shoppers Battle Wind 1964

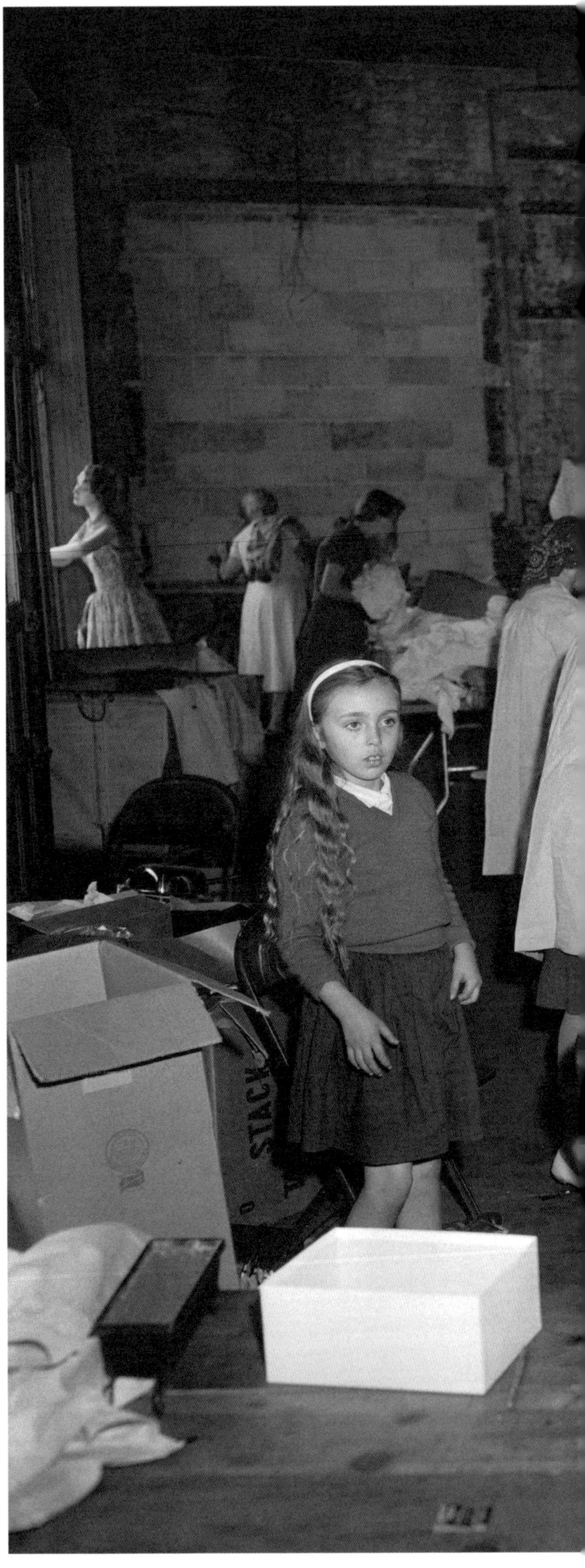

Harris School Rummage Sale, Chicago

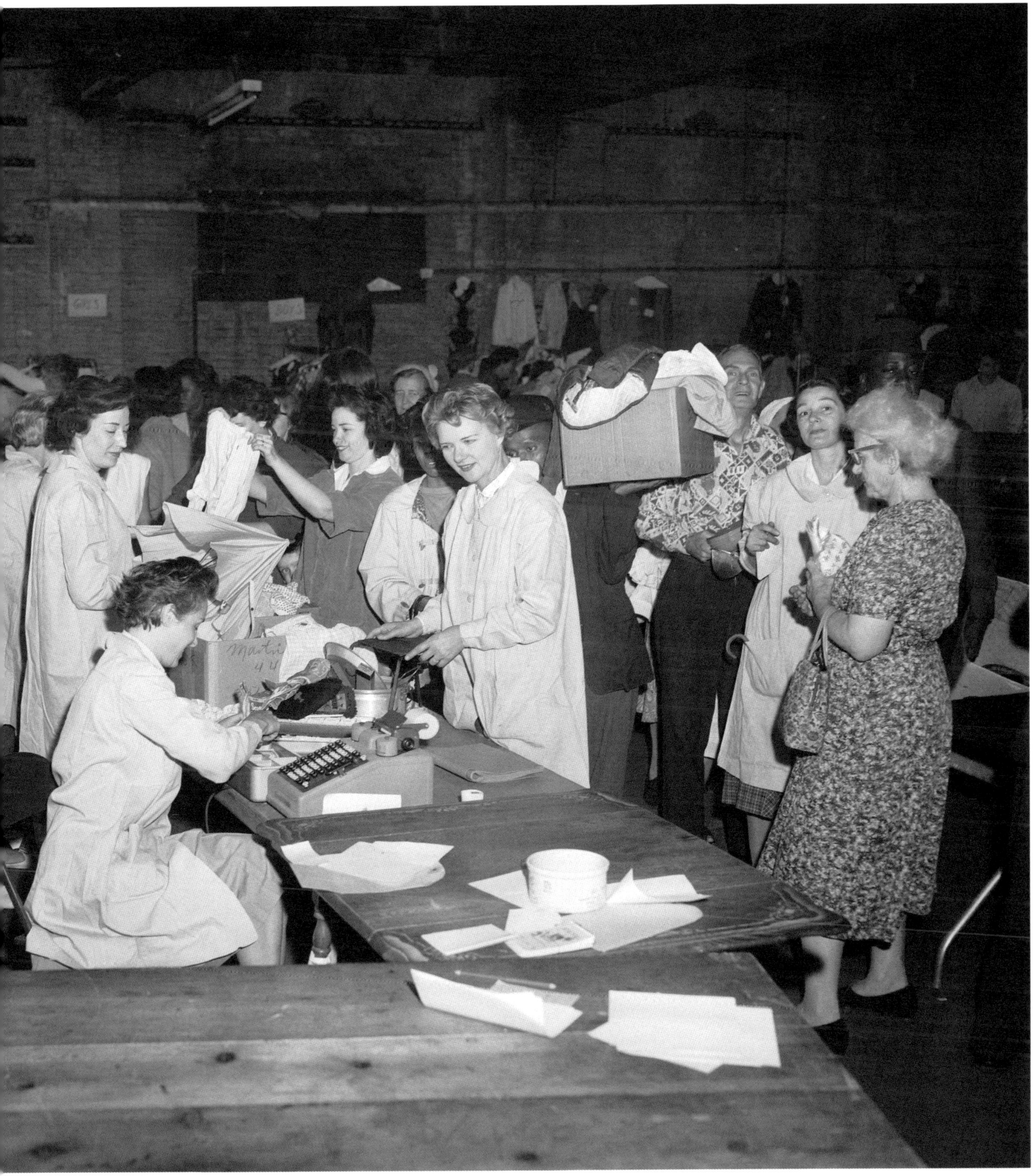

1961

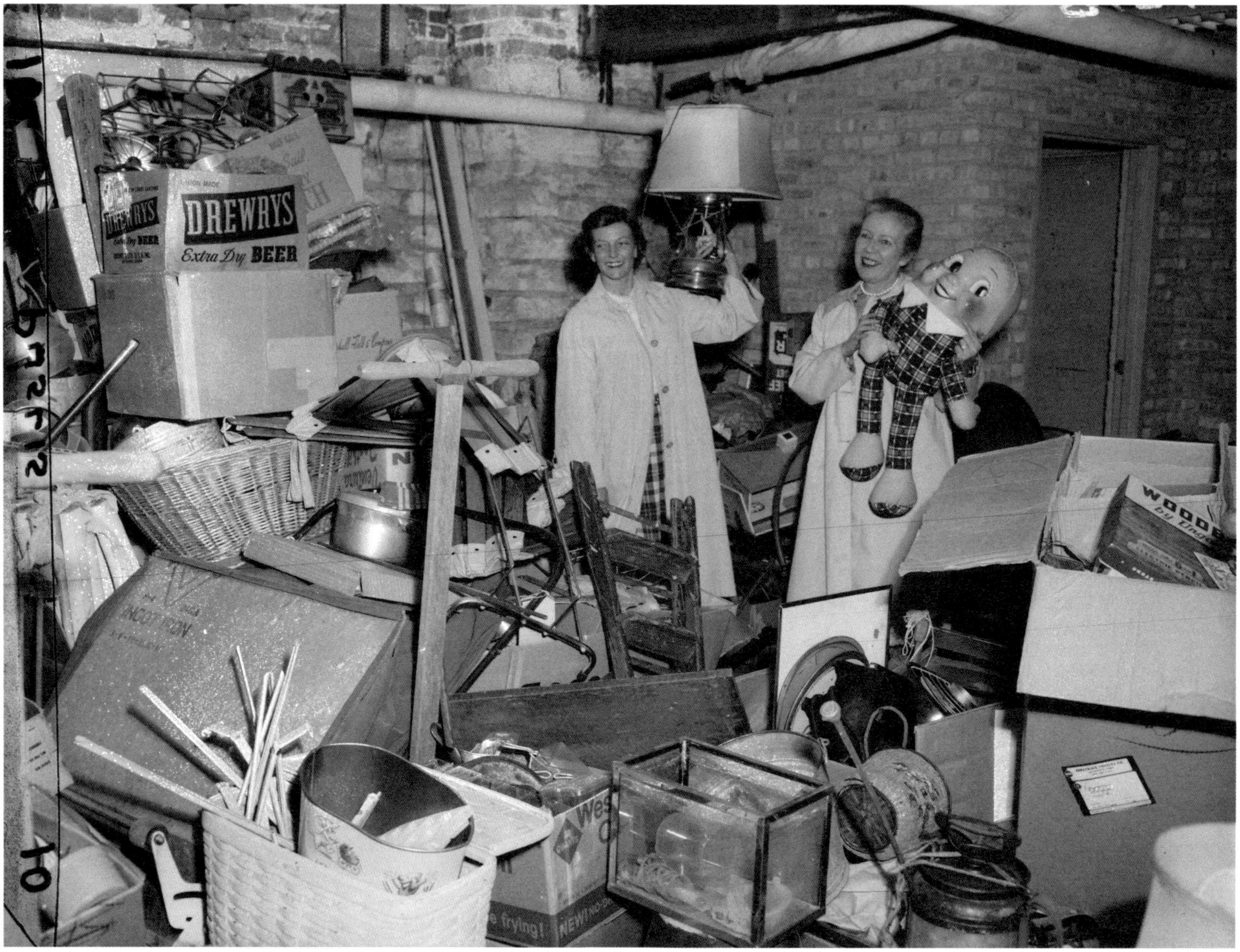

Congregational Church Rummage Sale, Winnetka, Illinois 1960

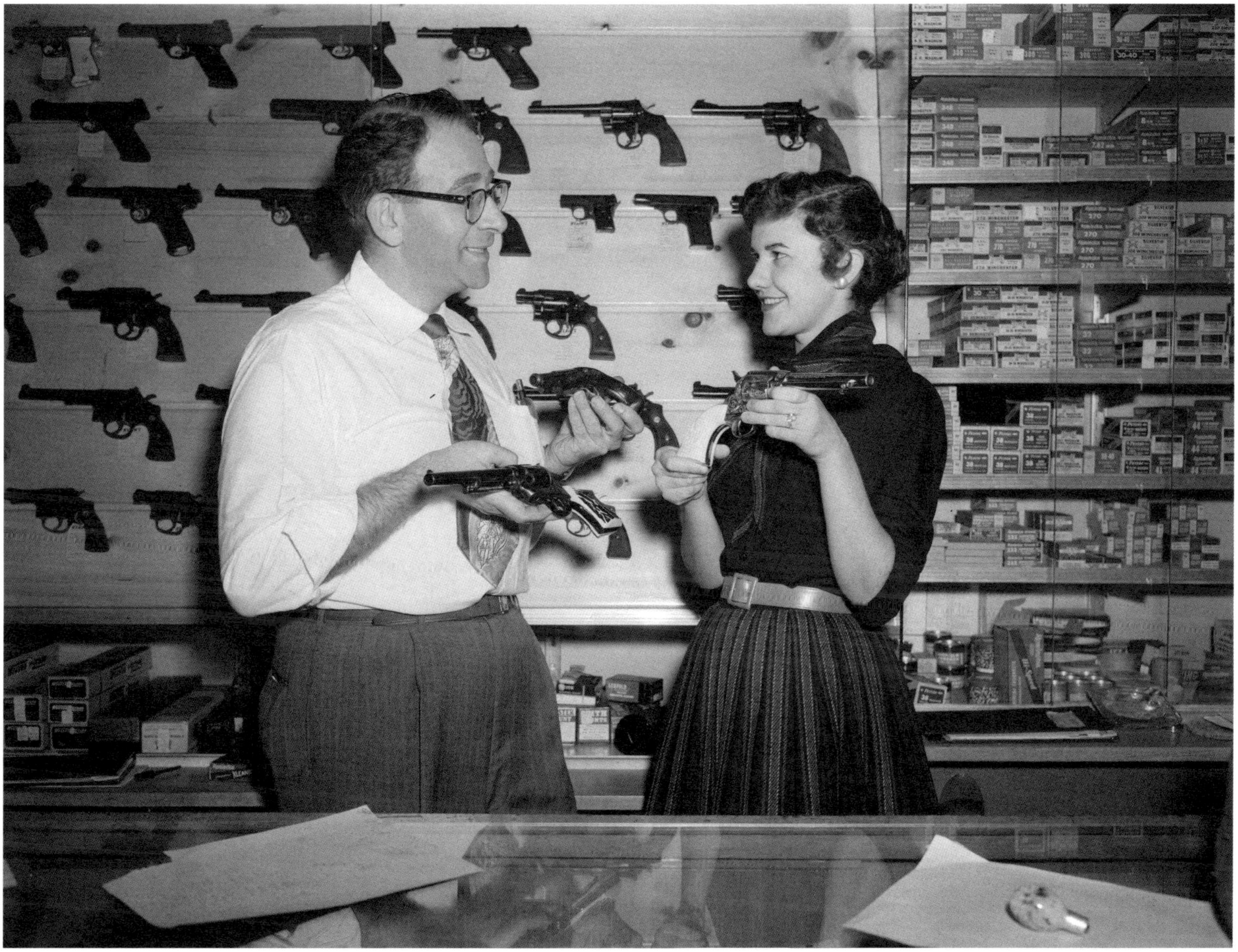

Antique Gun Traders, Chicago 1954

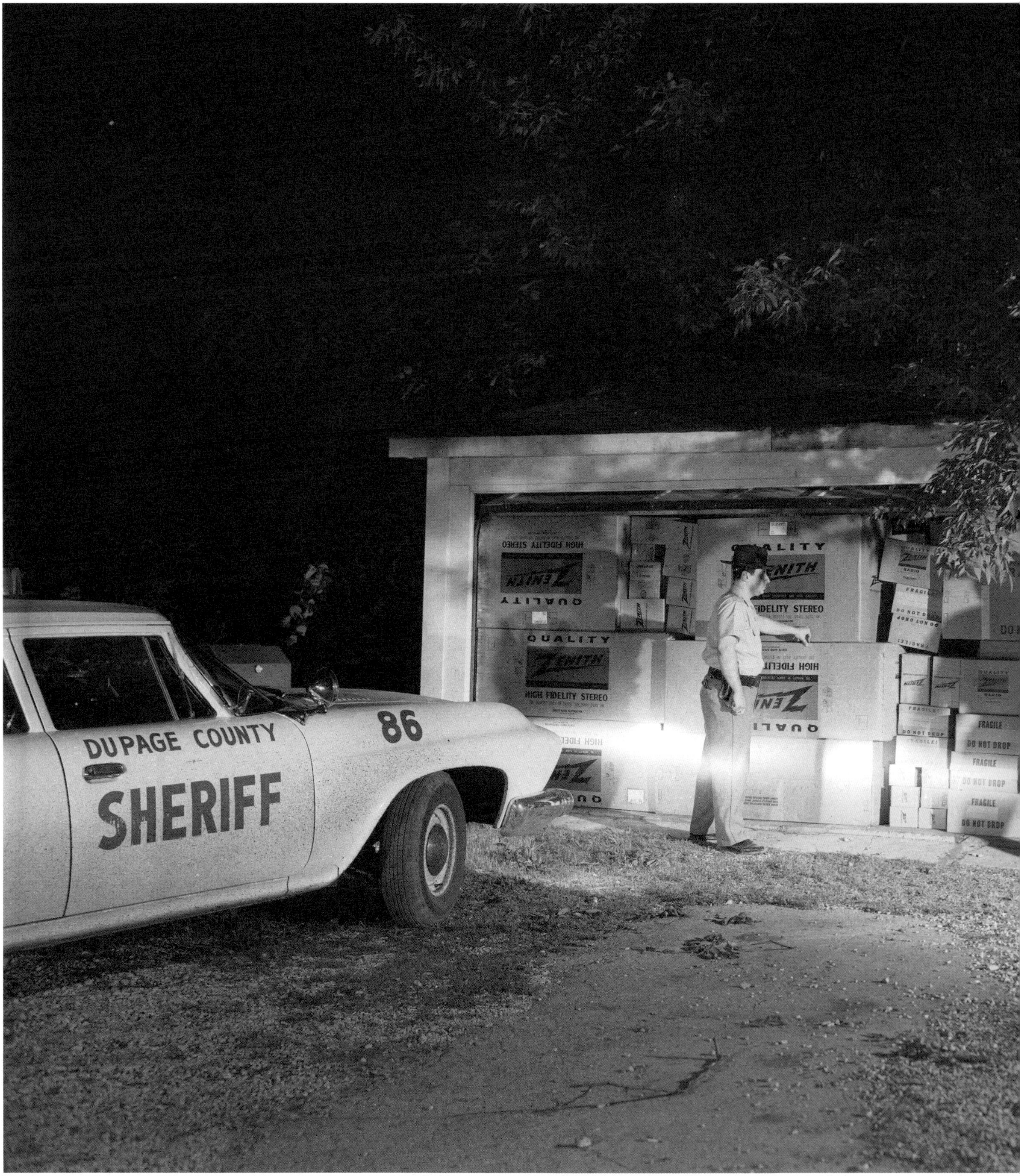

Cook County Sheriff Finds Stolen TVs

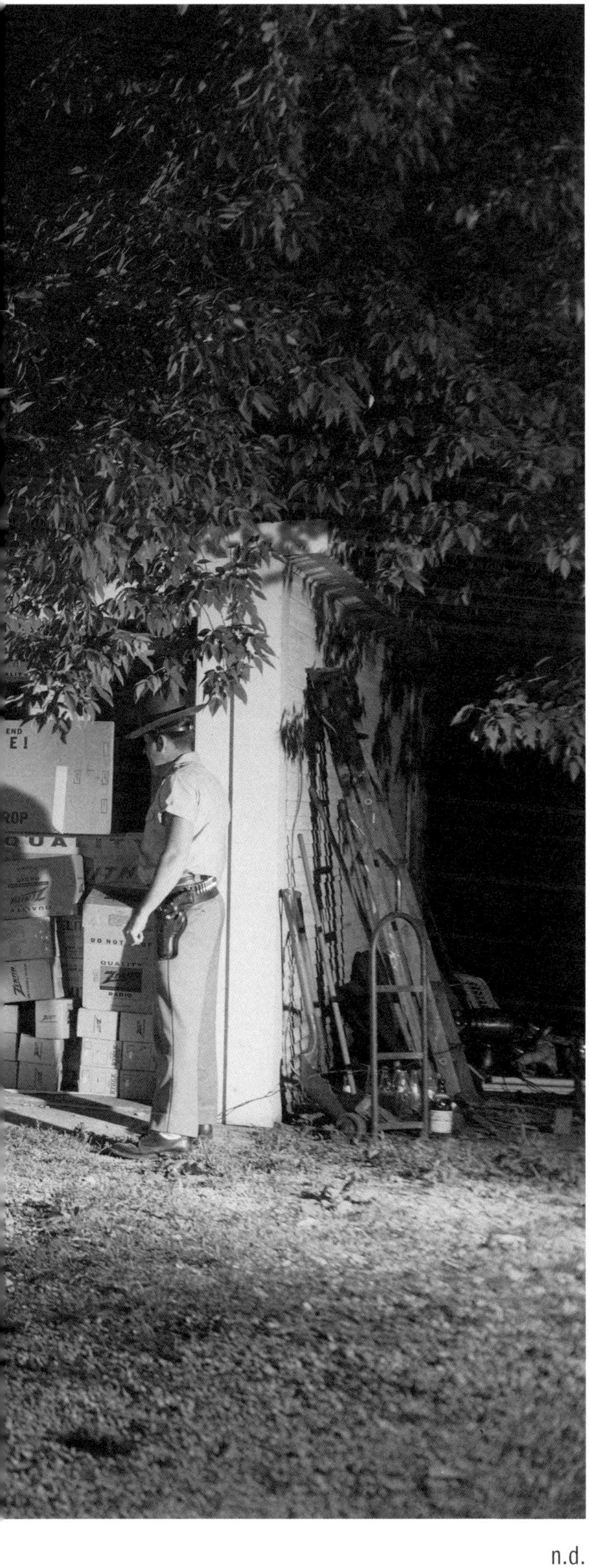

n.d.

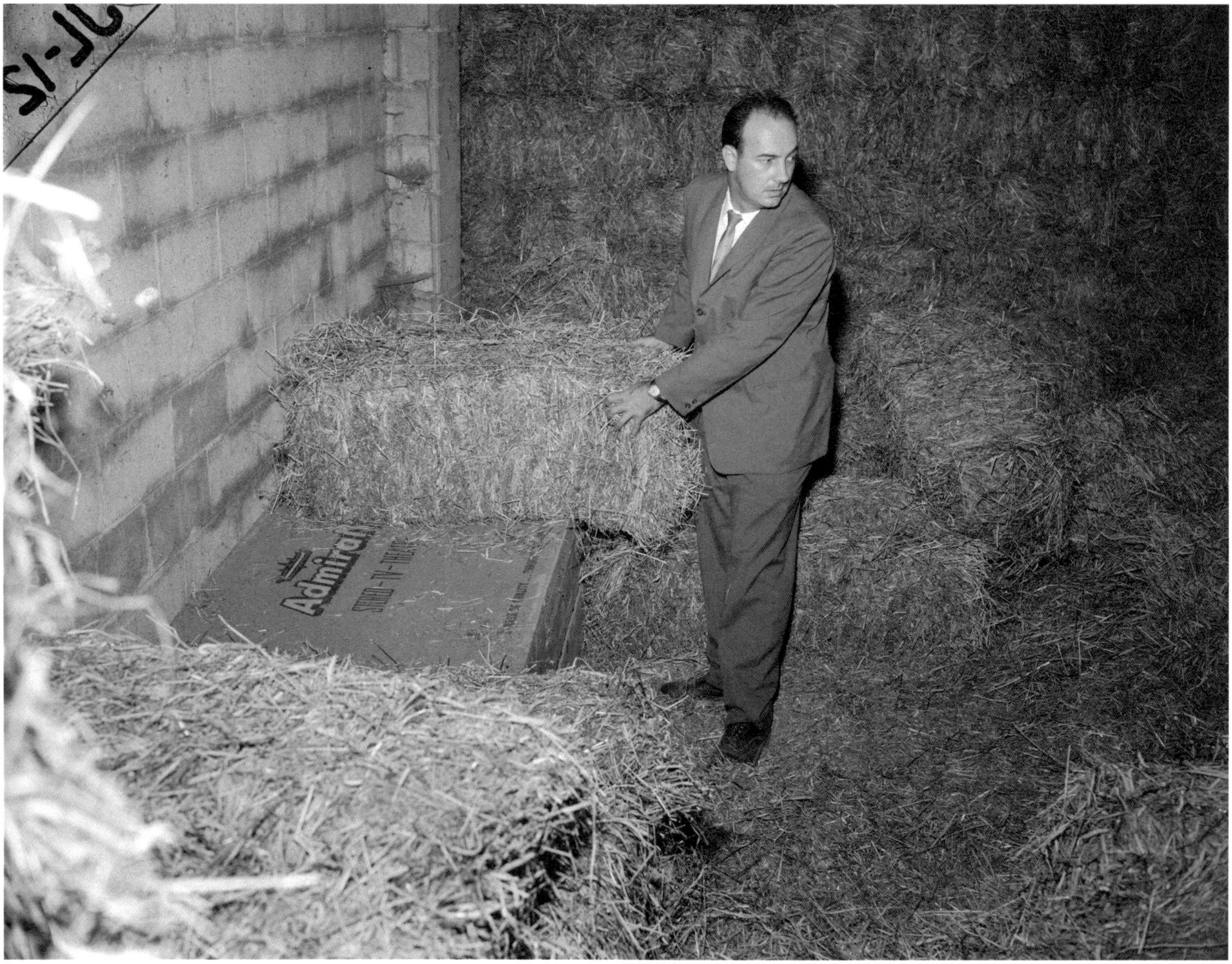

Admiral Phonograph Stolen From Store n.d.

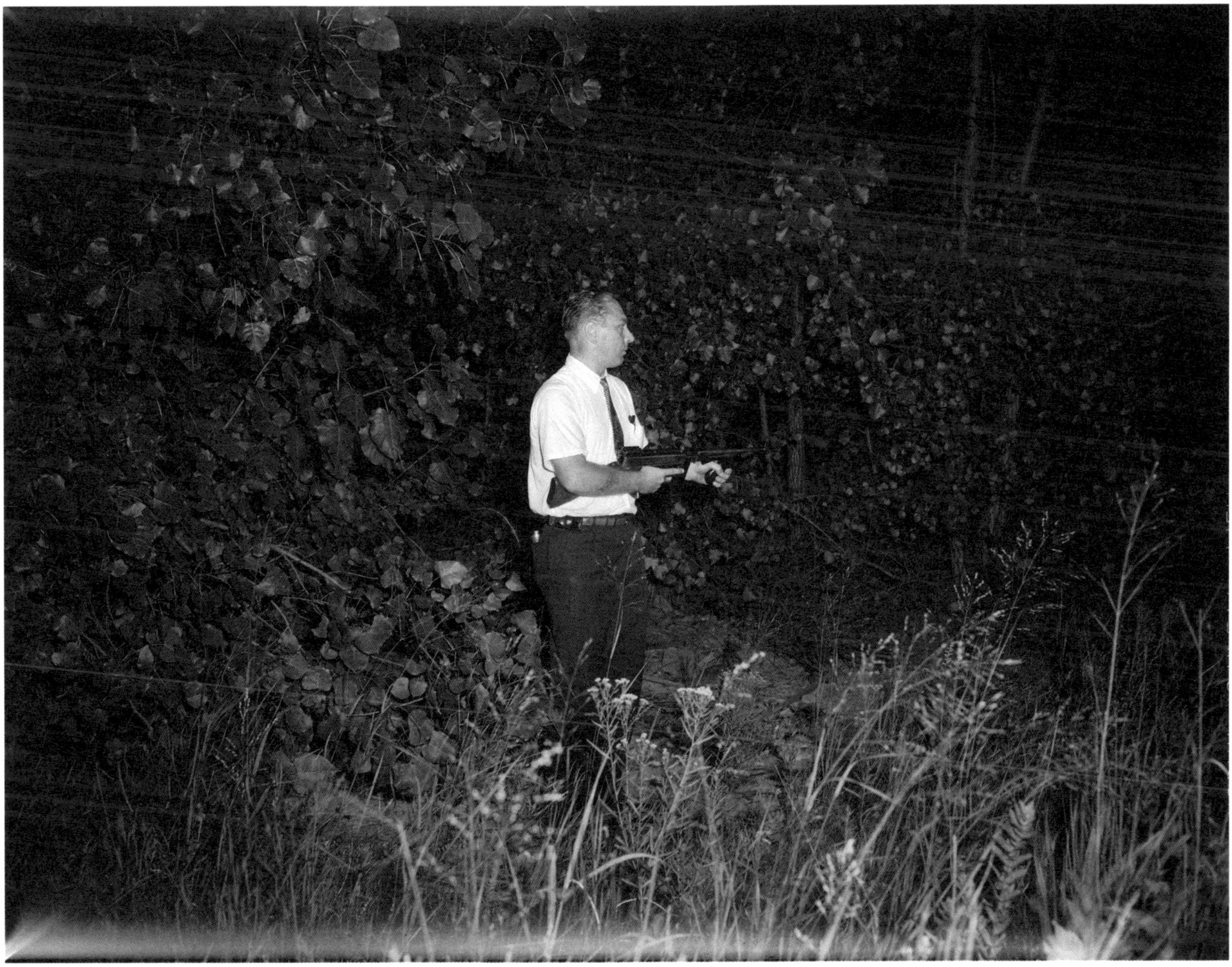

Robbery, Fairway Supermarket, Chicago 1958

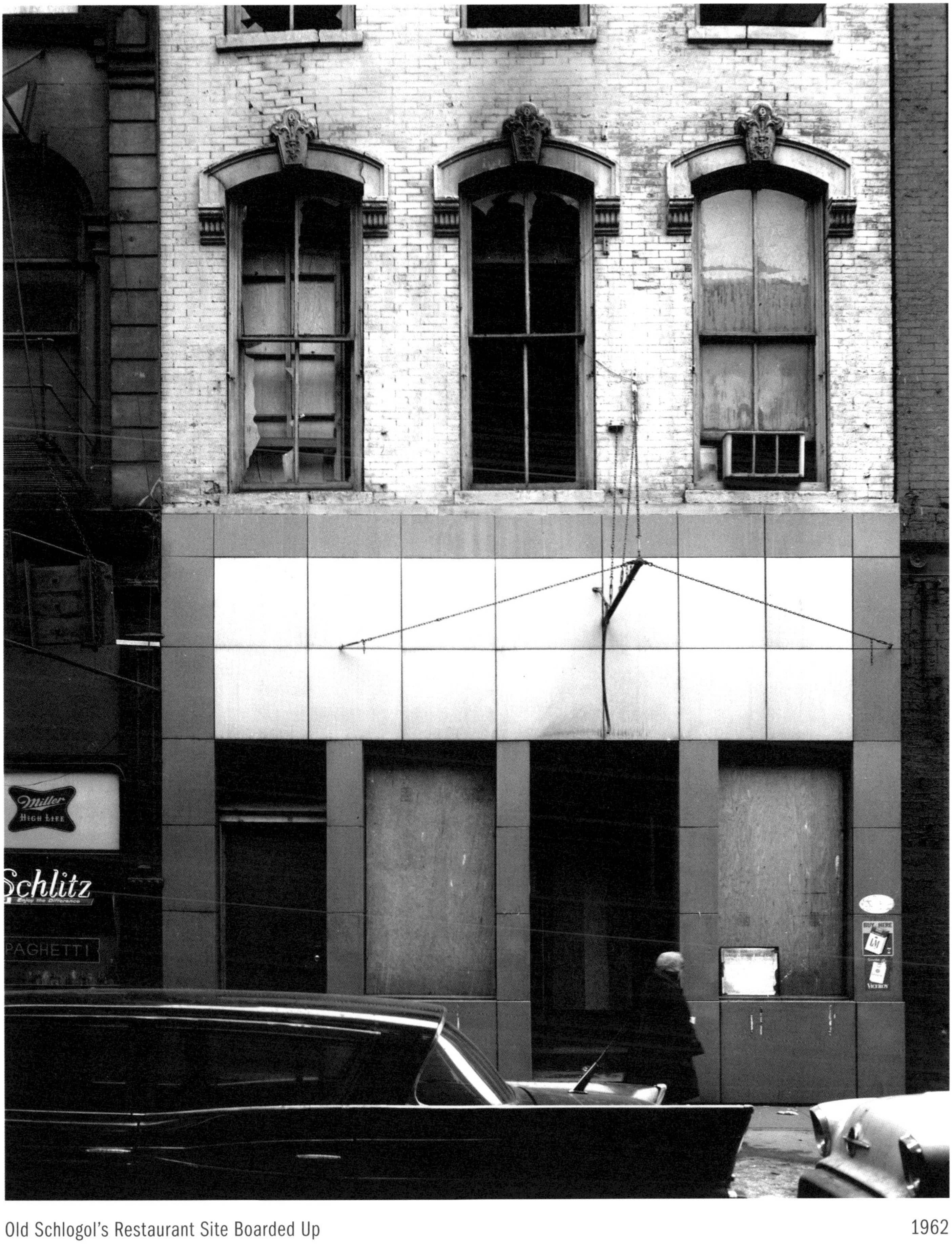

Old Schlogol's Restaurant Site Boarded Up 1962

I never think that people die.
They just go to department stores.

Andy Warhol

INTRODUCTION

Ashley Kistler

While Brian Ulrich is already widely known as an accomplished photographer, this book and the exhibition it accompanied reveal other aspects of his art-making that have evolved over the last four years. On a few earlier occasions, Ulrich had displayed several items from his personal archive in combination with his own photographs. The numerous images and objects featured in *Close Out: Retail Relics and Ephemera*, however, constituted the first presentation to take an in-depth look at his collecting activities. Opening concurrently at the Anderson Gallery with the traveling exhibition *Copia—Retail, Thrift, and Dark Stores*, Ulrich's decade-long investigation of American consumer culture, it also offered an initial opportunity to examine more closely how his approaches to photography and collecting intersect.

In creating a record of consumer culture through the three series and nearly 60 photographs making up *Copia*, Ulrich has likened his method of looking to that of an anthropologist.[1] His patient observation of retail sites, both populated and abandoned, has yielded incisive images that astutely distill the proclivities and many other aspects of human behavior engendered by a consumer-driven lifestyle. His impulse to collect retail artifacts—signage, documents, press photos, old credit cards, and much more—partakes in this investigation, too, providing a correlative route to understanding an immensely complicated set of issues.

As Ulrich observes in the interview that follows, his interest in sifting through these gritty relics grew in tandem with his development of the *Dark Stores* series—pursuits that apparently have been mutually reinforcing. Describing in an earlier statement the character of the seemingly inconsequential and discarded objects he salvages, Ulrich mentions the gravitas they gain in their new context of abandonment.[2] He allows this sensibility to also permeate his depictions of dark stores and dead malls, transforming otherwise quotidian, dispirited subjects into ghostly presences that rivet our attention. After all, as his photographs confirm, these buildings are now artifacts as well. Ulrich's typological treatment of certain groups of images in the series, which in some respects recall German photographers Bernd

1 "Brian Ulrich, Statement," *Is This Place Great or What, Photographs by Brian Ulrich* (New York: Aperture Foundation, in partnership with the Cleveland Museum of Art, 2011), n. pag.

2 Ibid.

and Hilla Becher's grids of dilapidated industrial structures, underscores this aspect; it also evinces a rapid, widespread phenomenon whose disastrous effects are likewise conjured by the contents of his archive.

The twinned themes embodied by two groups of photographs acquired by the artist and featured in the exhibition parallel in many respects the beginning and end points of the narrative arc charted in *Copia*. The earlier group—an extensive newspaper cache of negatives documenting the Great Prosperity, the post-World War II period of unprecedented growth for America's middle class—also extends this trajectory by making clear that what Ulrich began to record in 2001 has a much longer history. He regards these images as a prequel to his own work. Expressing a deep desire to make beautiful photographs that otherwise would have been badly printed and poorly reproduced if even seen at all, he accords them a level of attention reserved for his own picture-making and applies the same measured editorial eye.

In the two dozen Great Prosperity prints prepared for the *Close Out* exhibition, Ulrich teases out subtleties and nuance by considering with the utmost care every aspect of their production and presentation, including the sequence in which we encounter the pictures, as is also evident in the first section of this book. Using a specially selected paper stock, he opted to magnify each of three scenesinto gorgeous 40-by-50-inch renditions. While his resuscitation of these long-buried images greatly enhances their formal qualities, Ulrich's efforts are once again focused on a larger goal: the compilation of a more fully fleshed and captivating narrative that keenly reflects the era's burgeoning investment and faith in a consumer-driven culture. The underlying and prescient themes brought to light in these rescued documents help to further illuminate factors contributing to our current economic predicament, so compellingly explored in his *Copia* project.

As already suggested, Ulrich's facility to discern which artifacts potentially afford the greatest insights correlates with his ability as a photographer to cull and compose the most telling images from an always infinite number of possibilities. This is, in itself, a creative act, especially when confronted with the countless choices embedded in endless mounds of cast-off consumer detritus. A group of many hundreds of Polaroids depicting shoplifters, salvaged by Ulrich from the demolition of a local mall, offers another case in point. Intended to function like mug shots, and originally labeled with each culprit's name, social security number, and crime, they more readily resemble blurry, candid snapshots whose hapless subjects span divisions of gender, generation, and race. As always, Ulrich adapts his mode of presentation to focus attention on salient aspects of the items displayed. For *Close Out*, recognizing the inherent power of these images to speak to a range of issues, he simply arranged 96 of the Polaroid portraits in a long grid. As we consider them as they were originally displayed in a freestanding case, the matter-of-factness of their presentation only serves to accentuate the economic and societal tragedy that this slice of America represents.

Assembled as yet another typology indicative of our times, these pictures evoke one consequence of the so-called Great Regression, which witnessed increasing levels of income disparities during the 1980s and 90s; at the same time, as manifest in Ulrich's Great Prosperity images, they underscore just how successfully the previous era manufactured and exalted desire as the indelible core of a consumer culture. The Polaroids could also signify the penultimate event in a narrative that concludes, for now, with the multitude of dead malls rendered by Ulrich in *Copia*. This desolate, encroaching landscape and the artifacts that he has retrieved from it suggest Warhol's quip may not be as timely as it once was.

Ashley Kister is Director of the Anderson Gallery at the School of the Arts, Virginia Commonwealth University in Richmond.

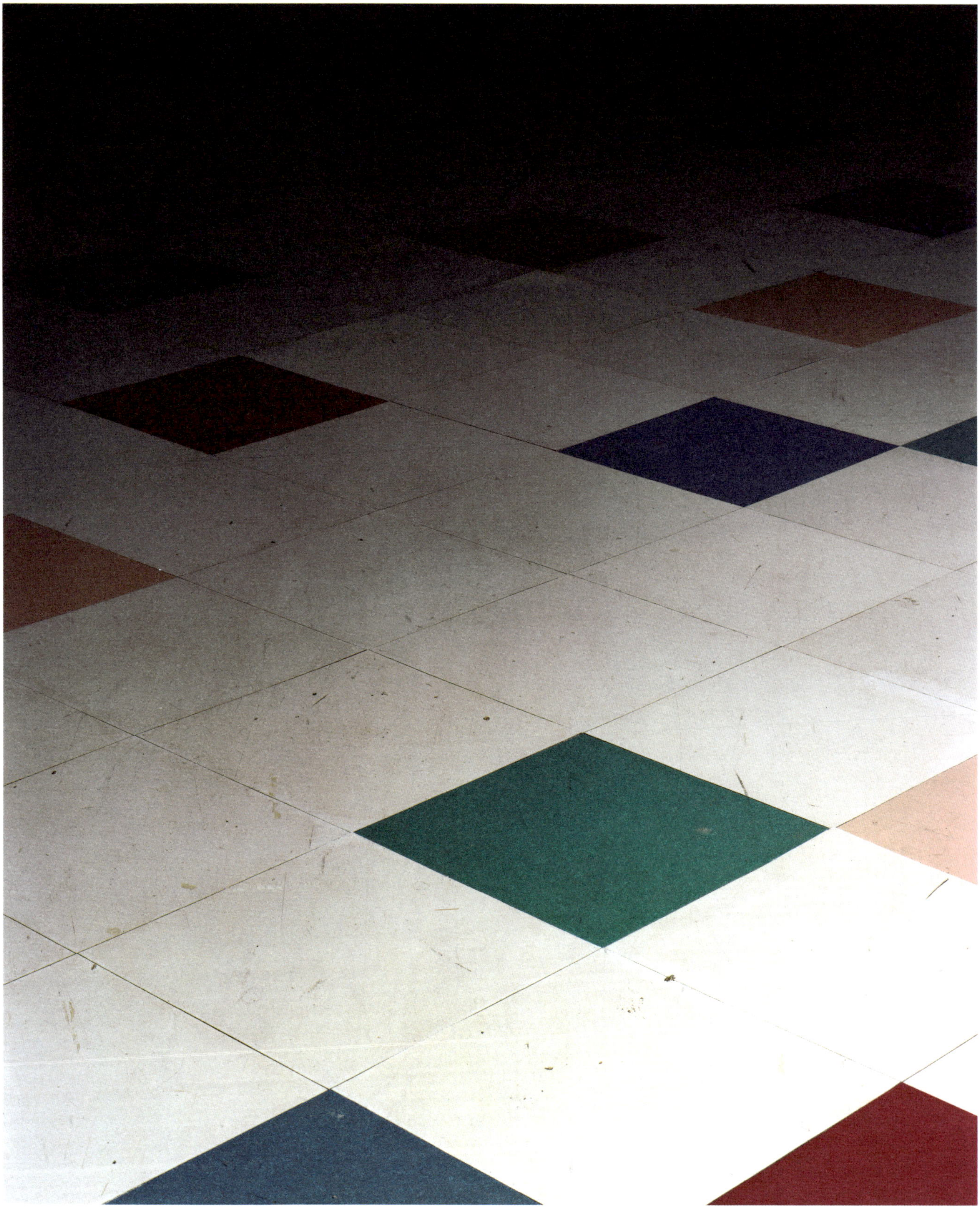

Brian Ulrich, *Marshall Fields 2,* 2009
From the series *Dark Stores, Ghostboxes & Dead Malls*

AK This may sound a little disparaging to ask, but is it fair to call you a dead-mallrat?

BU It depends on what you mean. [laughs] There's a large subculture of people who are really interested in the phenomenon of the dead mall, who have a vast amount of knowledge about this weird area of retail history and share it through Facebook, websites, online forums. One of these enthusiasts, Jon Revelle, has been called a dead-mallrat because he's known for literally crawling through a mall's infrastructure—walls, ceilings, basements—to find things. Jon is one of the people who led me to the first cache of mall-office ephemera at Dixie Square Mall, south of Chicago. A little crawl space had somehow survived a fire and contained all this random paperwork that we rummaged through for a day, gleaning what we could.

More important, though, was the realization that no one was around in those abandoned, derelict places to tell me not to take pictures. I could just continue to work. It was kind of a wonderful victory. The portion of my *Copia* project dealing with dead stores really became a lot of fun. It was actually hard to stop. My list still includes a number of places I'd like to either visit or return to, but it's an endless project that could go on forever.

AK Since your scavenging has advanced your image-making as well as your collecting interests, I assume these two pursuits have taken place in tandem with one another over the past few years?

BU Yes.

AK As you've become more familiar with dead-mall lore, you mentioned being able to zero in more quickly on where to look for the most interesting things. At a recently shuttered mall in this area, didn't you head first for the promotional files?

BU Yes, you start to figure out some strategies. At the Dixie Square Mall, piles upon piles of paper and folders had already been partially looked through by other people. And you only have so much time; I was precariously balanced on a rotten floor above a ceiling. So you're trying to work quickly and figure out which items might yield something about the history of the place and evoke a narrative. Certain files contained plans and maps, along with economic assessments for the design and its implementation, which are really interesting visually and shouldn't just end up in a dumpster.

Promotional files are always intriguing because they're essentially propaganda. In my own images, I've tried to underscore the fact that once advertising gimmicks are revealed, any kind of power just washes away. You'll also find photographs in these files. During the demolition of the local mall you mentioned, I found lots of negatives and prints that the mall had taken of competing malls for their own research, whether or not the same management company owned the other sites. I discovered all these great correlations with what I had been thinking about and doing.

AK So your interest in collecting these items is not only to explore how they establish the narrative of one particular place, but also to reveal how they illuminate a much larger story, much like your own photographs?

BU Ultimately, I'm trying to co-opt the material and re-contextualize it. That's the difficult, tricky part. Sometimes the literal aspect of a thing works, and other times it needs to be transformed in some way so that it represents something larger than itself. That's what photography does as well, right? I like playing with both of those elements: literal presence and narrative potential.

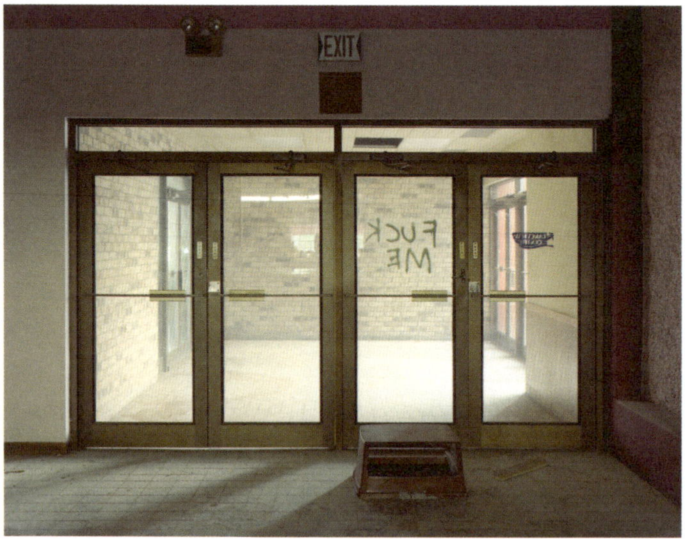

Brian Ulrich, *Mid Cities Mall*, 2011
From the series *Dark Stores, Ghostboxes & Dead Malls*

AK Under what circumstances did your collecting begin, and how do you now regard this activity within the context of your overall artistic practice?

BU What's really exciting to me about being an artist is reaching a place where you trust your practice, which allows you to undertake things that have a certain degree of risk and uncertainty. Receiving a Guggenheim Fellowship in 2009 not only enabled me to spend a year making new work; I also decided that I would take this opportunity to pursue whatever other ideas arose.

At the time, I was trying to photograph a sign on the exterior of the Dixie Square Mall that said "City Life." Out of frustration, I realized that I couldn't just photograph it. Even though I could make the picture in a million different ways, the image wasn't really going to eviscerate the literal veneer of this dumb sign. What if I relight the sign, I wondered, and alter its context?

AK Relight it at the site in order to take a photograph of it?

BU Yeah, or treat it as a kind of performance to see what would happen. But instead I took the sign down one night at two in the morning, balancing on ladders with a friend, and then had a guy in Chicago make new neon bulbs for it.

I like the idea of powering the signs back up. It's like jump-starting an engine that's run out of gas—a metaphor for reinvesting capital in the economy. The light of the sign, of course, signifies that the place it marks is functioning and accessible. Turning it back on in a new context, I think, is really interesting.

AK What initially occurred when you experimented with this idea?

BU A few years ago, I exhibited the City Life sign with some of my *Dark Stores* photographs at the Art Chicago Fair. Later on, at the Julie Saul Gallery, I integrated a few more objects and ephemera, including a big Fast Food sign, with a selection of *Copia* pictures. The trick is to push and pull these two things into a relationship with each other that isn't just complementary but underscores the way narrative functions in an object vs. a photograph. Establishing those relationships has

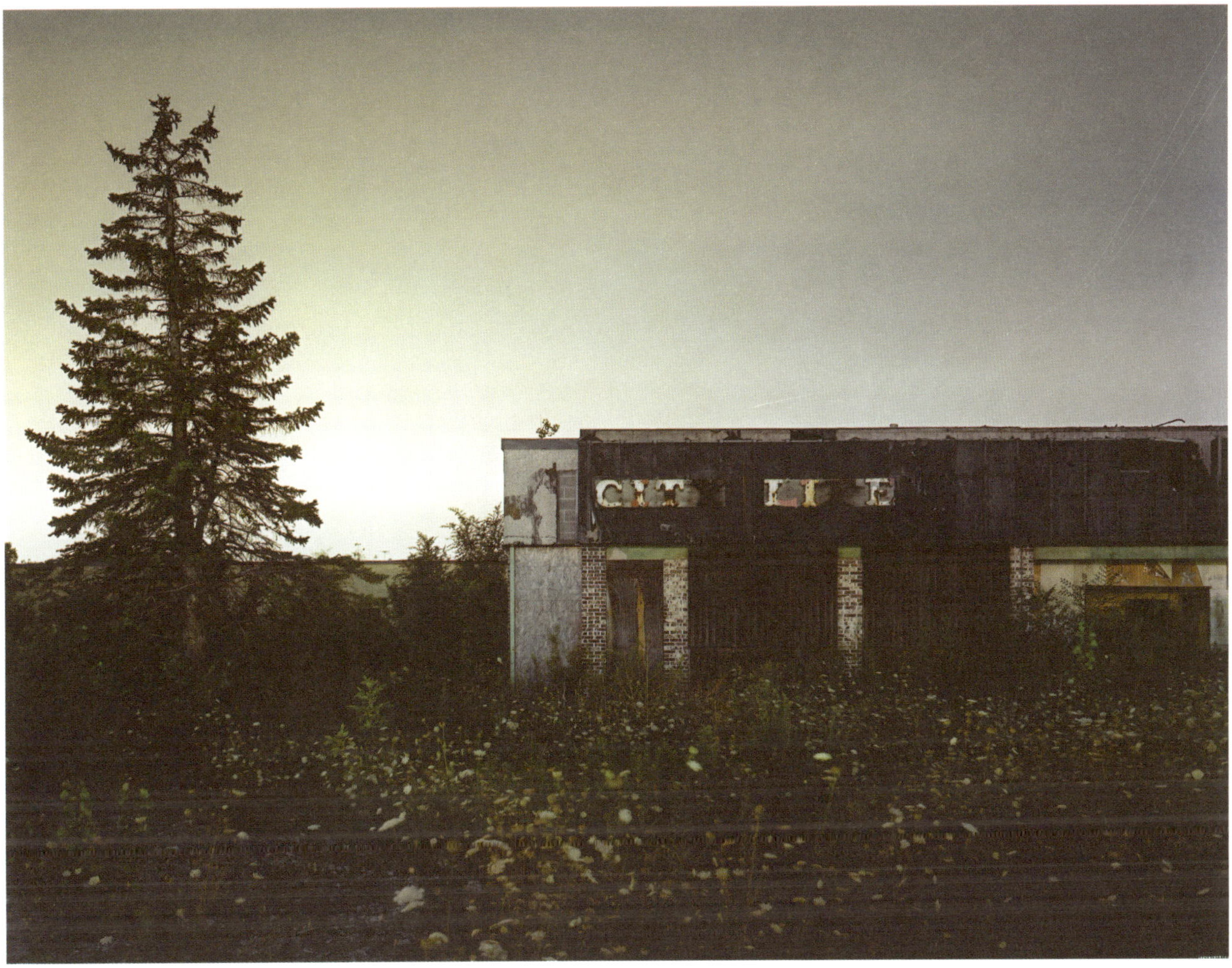

been the hard part; the sign too easily serves as an anecdote or remains a separate thing, competing with the photographs.

At the Anderson Gallery, however, we have a significant amount of space in which to work and experiment, as well as the contents of the entire *Copia* exhibition on the second floor. Those ten years of photographs map a time period and a trajectory, among other things, so it's easier to tease out relationships among the images rather than relying, for example, on the literal connection between a fast-food sign and fast-food photographs. I've spent a huge amount of time curating my purchase of film negatives from a press archive to tailor a narrative describing an economic period from the 1940s to the 1970s. The assembly of these pictures here will hopefully propel this idea while still preserving a degree of interest and ambiguity in each image and object that will pull people in.

AK What questions and dilemmas are foremost in your mind as you make decisions about the presentation of this material—the Great Prosperity photographs, as you call them.

BU The archive consists of four-by-five and sometimes two-and-a-quarter negatives, as well as a considerable number of prints, that I bought from private collectors on eBay. To me, the negatives are really interesting, mostly because they were never looked at.

Brian Ulrich, *City Life, Dixie Square Mall*, 2008. From the series *Dark Stores, Ghostboxes & Dead Malls*

Particularly appealing are those "wrong" moments that were captured, indecisive or unedited moments.

Almost all of the pictures were taken with a Speed Graphic press camera equipped with flash bulbs, which produces a very specific and, in my opinion, wonderful photographic language that goes well beyond our understanding of Weegee's street photographs, for instance. Armies of photographers were working this way. They would arrive on the scene to cover a story and take many pictures. The editor would pick just one image, which would be printed, cropped, half-toned, and reproduced at extremely low resolution.

Just scanning the original negatives and thinking about them as a kind of art photography, or in the context of my other work, is really powerful. Is it acceptable for me to scan another photographer's negative—even carefully, with a high-resolution drum scanner—reprint it, and call it my own? That's a really complicated question. So my other inclination was to mess with the images.

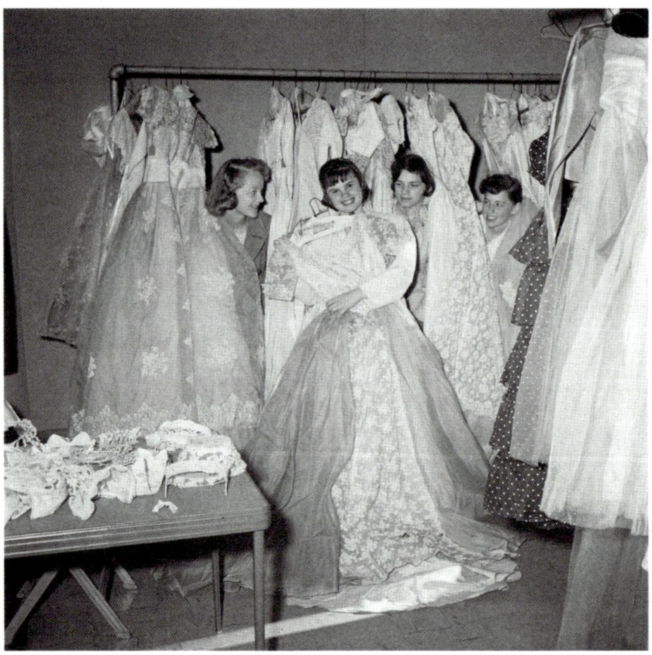

Congregational Church's Rummage Sale, Winnetka Community House, 1960
Print made from found negative

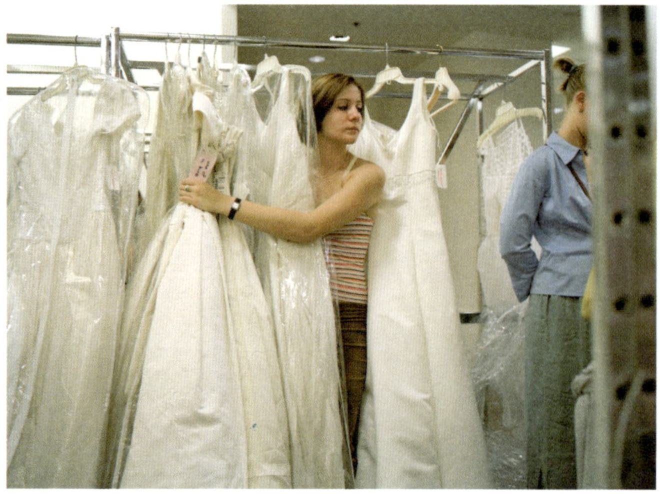

Brian Ulrich, *Chicago, IL*, 2003
From the series *Retail*

Can I re-appropriate them in a more experimentally aesthetic or formal way? Because the pictures are already loaded with a wonderful narrative, I ultimately decided I couldn't compete with that. The clown shaking hands with the four businessmen under the Jewel sign, for example, is so good that it simply needs to be re-contextualized.

AK You're accomplishing this in other ways, too, like re-sizing the printed image or, through your own editorial process, configuring selected photographs in purposeful sequences and arrangements.

BU Photography is such a complex phenomenon. The language of photography can be really overwhelming but also extremely profound in its ability to communicate immediately with vast audiences. An immensely complex event happens in that little square or rectangle.

AK You've been teaching students and other individuals how to look at photographs for some time now. How does an installation like this help to promote an understanding of the medium's language?

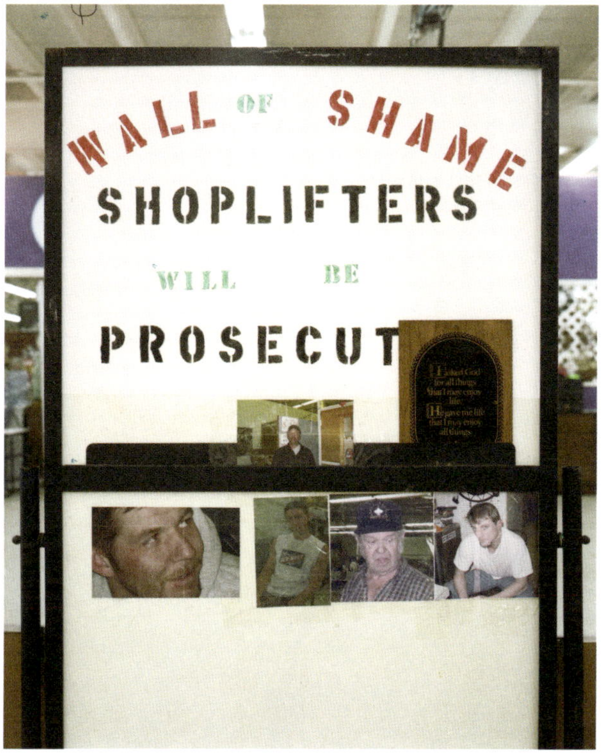

those pictures in the context of the *Copia* show because you realize a narrative's at play that's been going on for a long time.

And it's completely by design. I read a story about Black Friday the other day. A woman who works at Walmart sided with fellow employees who protested the store's opening on Thanksgiving since they couldn't be with their families. But then there she was shopping at Walmart because the holiday sales were too good to pass up. She didn't really seem to know what else to do with herself. It wasn't much different in 1948, when people no longer needed to be frugal for the war effort and instead were running through the doors of new stores that couldn't open fast enough.

BU With the *Copia* project, I didn't necessarily set out to produce this vast ten-year anthem; but once I realized that I was on a path, it became clear to me that I could create an evolving relationship among all the photographs, and that the addition of new pictures would alter the meaning of the earlier ones. The viewer is allowed to swim in this wonderful pool of information that teaches you about photography—the correlations that occur between mundane details, the way a lens reproduces a three-dimensional scene and renders light, how pictures establish connections that otherwise would not surface, and so on.

The difficult part of the archive pictures is that it is easy for them to exist as nostalgic. If you're looking at a picture that shows what it was like to buy something in 1950, you don't experience the same visceral reaction that a contemporary image of a comparable scene evokes. But something like this can happen by viewing

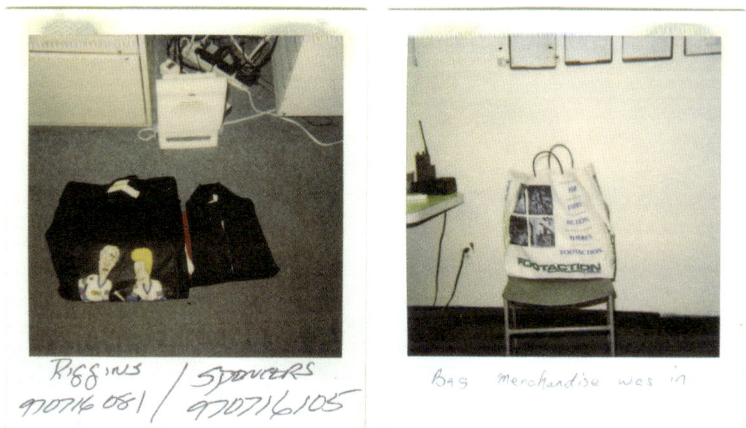

AK Let's carry this narrative thread through to the other body of photographs in *Close Out*—the Polaroids of shoplifters arrested for crimes and banned from mall property. Would you talk about the content of these images and how they relate to the wider narrative arc you're examining?

BU The Polaroids are pictures of people who were arrested for stealing or writing bad checks and sometimes for indecent exposure, drug use, or

Brian Ulrich, *Untitled 0721*, 2007
From the series *Thrift*

Found Polaroids, 2012

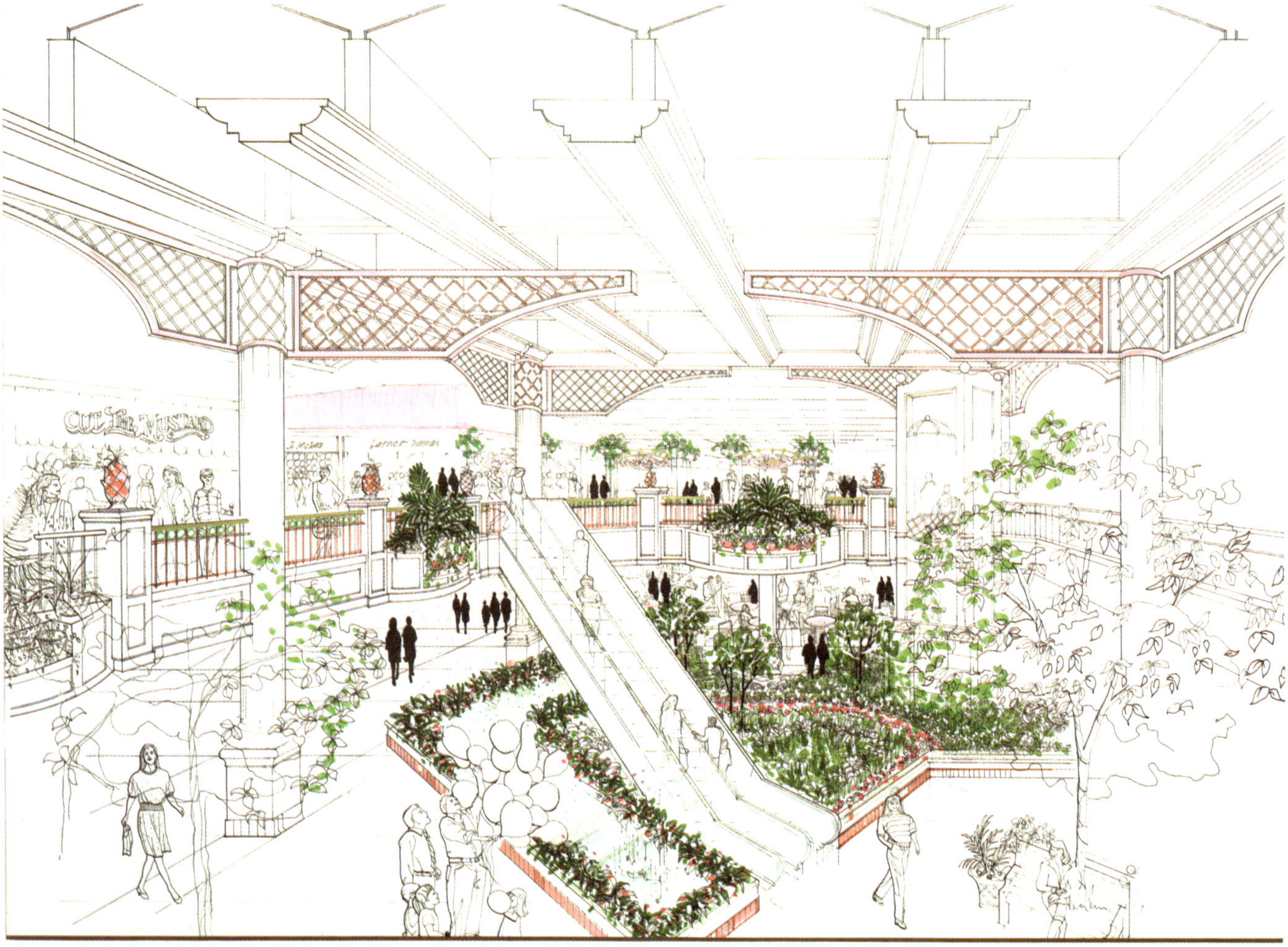

prostitution. But they're much more complex than what they literally depict. When I found the photographs, I just had to hold on to them, though I didn't know what I would do with them. After spending time really thinking about these pictures in terms of this project and what they ultimately represent, I realized once again that they were not only important to a specific time period but also evoked something potentially much larger.

When I considered the Polaroids of shoplifters in relation to the Great Prosperity pictures, I realized they represent the flipside—what some economists call the Great Regression. In contrast to the economic expansion of the Great Prosperity, this period was marked by the erosion of all the federally-funded programs that had been put in place to support middle-class growth. The Polaroids suggest that the manufacture of desire during the post-World War II era was so powerful and profound that people were willing to give up their moral codes to attain things. The most interesting aspect of these pictures is not just the fact that the individuals portrayed weren't able to afford something; they're about wanting something so badly that you're willing to steal and get arrested for it.

Along the same lines, the *Copia* exhibition includes a photograph I made at a thrift store in Chehalis,

JC Penney Court, Rolling Acres Mall, 2012
Checklist 5

Washington. It shows a propaganda poster with the heading "wall of shame" above photographs of people busted for stealing, each picture with its own wonderfully weird language.

AK How have you applied these strategies of re-presentation—especially as noted with the Great Progression images—to the architectural renderings featured in the exhibition?

BU The drawing of the JC Penney court at the Rolling Acres Mall court is pretty faithful to what was actually built, although they did opt for palm trees, as you pointed out, which are way more exotic. [laughs] I used to go to this mall when I lived in Akron. I found the drawing a year after I'd photographed the court, which by then had closed, from nearly the same vantage point. It seemed to be the obvious picture to make, with the escalator surrounded by empty, motionless space and overgrown greenery. There's a great, albeit fortuitous relationship between my picture and the drawing.

I've always thought about exhibiting the drawing, though I wasn't interested in it as an object; it was drawn on this cheesy foam-core board. So I decided to photograph it with an eight-by-ten-inch view camera and make a large-scale print that reinforces the content of the drawing—the really poor scale as well as the bounding optimism and even a kind of salvation that it's supposed to represent.

This also applies to the Dixie Square Mall image and my interest in it, though I worked from a found, eight-by-ten-inch copy negative that was made of a drawing for promotional purposes. The negative was really quite damaged, so I scanned and restored some of it, but I also left a lot of the damage.

AK As if to physically obliterate some of that feigned optimism, particularly in light of Dixie Square's troubled history?

BU Yeah, the damage in the image appears like a dark cloud. People argue that the mall was cursed, with problem after problem. With huge fanfare and financial investment, its opening coincided with the implementation of busing programs to make schools in the suburbs around Chicago more racially diverse. This instigated the phenomenon of white flight, which quickly transformed the surrounding middle-class neighborhood into a site of racial and political unrest. When the larger and fancier Lincoln Mall opened fifteen miles away, what little economy was left in Dixie Square was sucked away.

AK Besides the two bodies of photographs and related paper ephemera, the exhibition also includes various objects. Why do these items appeal to you, and how are you addressing their presentation?

BU There's an installation of ten aluminum door-pulls from Montgom-

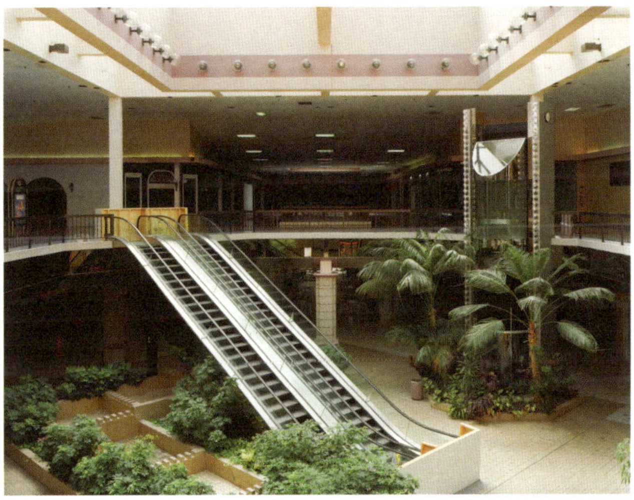

Brian Ulrich, *Rolling Acres Mall*, 2008
From the series *Dark Stores, Ghostboxes & Dead Malls*

ery Ward, a company whose story I love because it's synonymous with American retail mythology. It started out as a mail-order business in the late-nineteenth century—the company's catalogue was popularly called the "Wish Book"—and later opened hundreds of outlet stores across the country, competing with Sears and other retailers. The company was bought and restructured by Mobil in the 1970s, but then died a slow death, resulting in the largest retail bankruptcy liquidation in U.S. history.

The door-pulls came from a mall in Manitowoc, Wisconsin. They're beautiful objects, with a level of detail rarely seen anymore. Everything is made to be so disposable today. A recessed "M" on top is simply flipped over to become a "W" on the bottom. I love the idea that you literally grabbed the logo to open the door to the store.

AK The design and implementation of the logo are pretty subtle by today's standards.

BU Yeah, they're not bombastic. I decided to arrange the door-pulls in a linear, uniform way—almost like a sideways Donald Judd sculpture. I'm certainly co-opting this language from Judd, but not to establish a relationship with his work. I want instead to encourage viewers to look at them aesthetically, as art objects.

Also included in the show is a 1980s tape machine manufactured by Customusic, one of Muzak's competitors. I'm curious about the conspiracy-theory thinking that must shape a strategy like Muzak—that is, music meant to influence spending—as if creating a certain kind of environment with a particular soundtrack would compel consumers to want to own a thing even more and rip money out of their pockets because… a horn version of a Rod Stewart song is playing over the sound system. [laughs]

AK Yes, this exhibition is not without humor! Your salvaged Art for Less electric sign, which will be mounted on the gallery's façade, certainly sets this tone as soon as visitors approach the building.

BU Yeah, that's important to a lot of the work. There's also humor and comedy in the archive images and their re-contextualization. The Muzak player is ridiculous, you know? It's ostentatious, over the top, and kind of ugly.

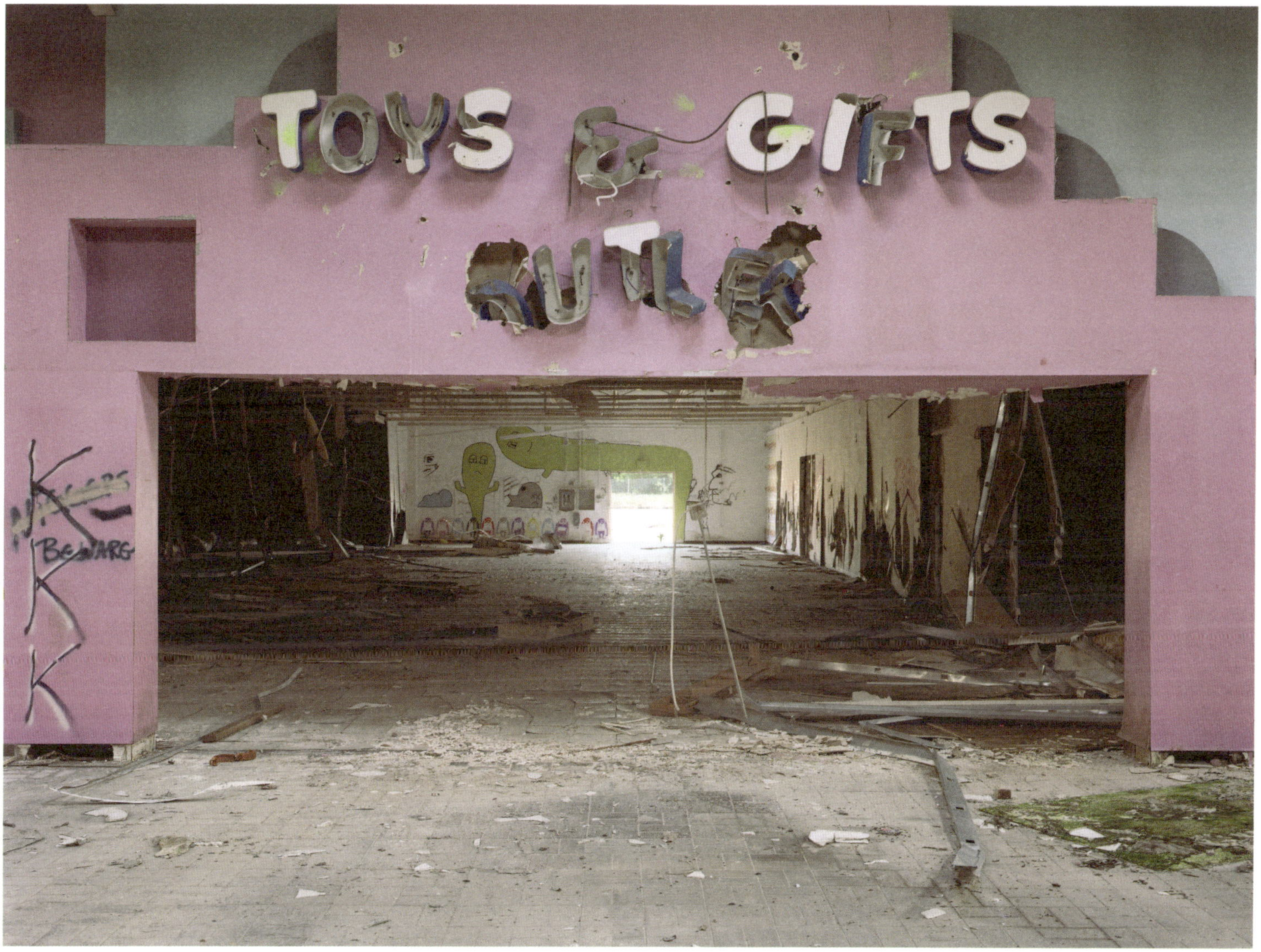

Brian Ulrich, *Toys & Gifts*, *Belz Factory Outlet Mall,* 2009. From the series *Dark Stores, Ghostboxes & Dead Malls*

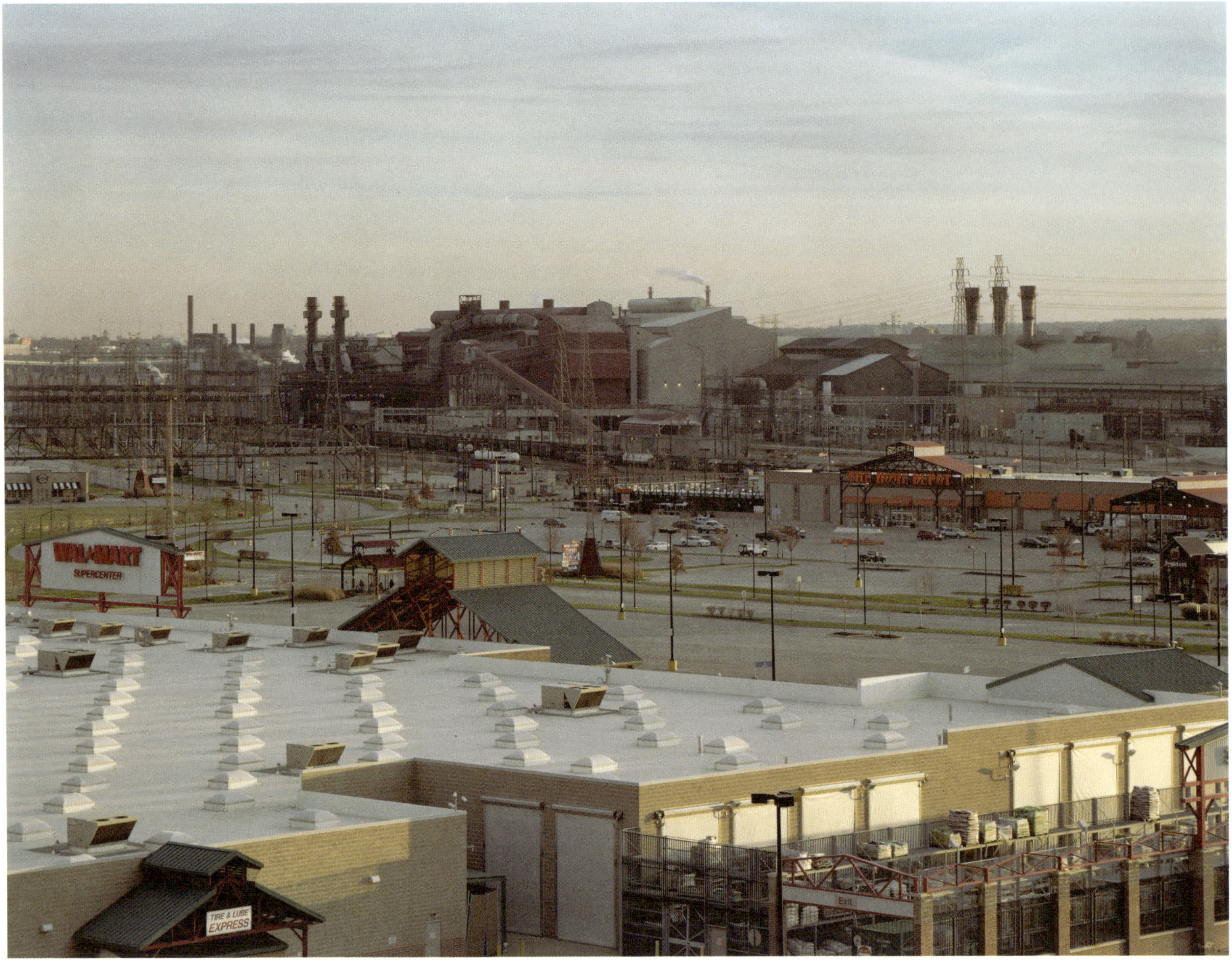

Brian Ulrich, *Steelyard Commons, Cleveland, OH*, 2011. From the series *Dark Stores, Ghostboxes & Dead Malls*

The current advertising slogan appearing under the blue letters that spell Walmart proclaims: "Save money. Live Better." America's largest employer certainly can't be referring to the lives of their 2.1 million full-time workers who earn $8.81 an hour. Or to the part-time employees who work less than 28 hours a week and therefore do not qualify for health care benefits or unemployment insurance should they be laid off in the post-holiday season. Or to the millions of sweatshop workers in emerging economies like India and China who work excessive hours to earn $37 a month, making those $4.96 "Rollback Savings" bath towels. And they most definitely cannot be talking about the 114 garment workers who died in a factory fire in December 2012 in Bangladesh, as a result of unregulated, unsafe work conditions eerily similar to New York's Triangle Waist Fire of 1911 that killed 146 workers. No, this little jingo can't be referring to them because that would be a lie. Unfortunately, we live in an era where unregulated free-market capitalism and a-get-rich-or-die quest for profits have eroded into social and moral bankruptcy. Selling lies keeps the cash registers ringing, increases executive bonuses year after year and, most importantly, always satisfies that ravenous shareholder hunger with a dividend feast. For the past 40 years, the American people have been sold a monstrous lie.

But it wasn't always like this. As a nation, we used to make things that the rest of the world consumed; now we are the world's largest consumer. America's economy didn't consist of high corporate profits, large dividend payouts, and low wages, and it wasn't solely dependent upon the consumer. From the end of World War II and into the early 1970s, America experienced a great economic boom in which prosperity and wealth grew from the middle outwards. From 1946 to 1973, U.S. GDP grew at an annual pace of 3.8% a year; real median household income surged 74% as earnings for the average male worker increased 25% each decade; and worker compensation rose at the same rate of productivity. In 1950, 35% of the private sector workforce was unionized, and so workers had the bargaining power to demand a 40-hour work week and a decent living wage as they shared the rewards of productivity growth, i.e. profits.

Within the past 40 years, annual earnings for the average male worker have fallen by 28%, and corporate profits as a percentage of GDP are currently at record highs. Today, private sector union membership is at 6.9% as factory jobs have declined by 40% since the early 1970s. From 2000–2010, the annual income of middle-class families shrank by $3,837. In 2010, middle-income families (those making $46,000) spent 91% of their after-tax income. In the next two decades, U.S. GDP is projected to grow at only 2.2%. Since 70% of our GDP is based on consumer-spending, economic growth is dependent upon wage earners having a steady paycheck, i.e. money to spend. When one hand does not feed the other, the cycle that defines our country's economy is broken. In a consumer economy, the greatest threat to our nation lies in the evisceration of the middle class.

As the result of globalization and the mechanization of the factory floor, the prospects for future job growth now exist in low-paying retail-service jobs. The Bureau of Labor Statistics estimates that 7 out of 10 new jobs over the next decade will be low-wage jobs, and the median wage for 80% of the workforce that is paid by the hour will continue to fall and thus send poverty rates up. Recent studies have shown that a single worker needs an average income of $30,012 a year to cover expenses and save for retirement. Our current federal government deficit is $16 trillion. As a nation, we must ask: how do we dig ourselves out of this mess when the government is obliged to take care of a retired baby-boom generation and provide a safety net for those living in poverty, as federal tax revenues and middle-class earnings continue to shrink while corporate profits and bonuses continue to surge? When considering the winners and losers here, one might ask who is left with the bill? We, the people are, while the CEOs and Fortune 500 companies sail away in their yachts, and we are left stranded on the shoreline screaming: whatever happened to corporate responsibility and patriotism?

The wealthiest companies in America have at the very least a moral obligation to provide their workers with a livable wage that keeps pace with the rate of inflation. The average full-time Walmart employee makes approximately $18,000 a year and, with these near-poverty wages, Walmart's own workers do not have the purchasing power to shop at Walmart. $8.18 does not go very far in today's economy when a gallon of gas costs $4; a gallon of milk is $3.50; and a McDonald's Big Mac meal is $6.50. In 1978, CEOs at the largest U.S. companies made on average 35 times the pay of the average worker. In 2010, CEOs made on average 343 times the pay of the average worker. The 46 million Americans living in poverty and the 103 million Americans living in near-poverty don't have the financial means to contribute any more to our consumer economy than they already are. And yet, if given just enough of an annual raise to boost them above the poverty line, our federal deficit would shrink as the number of people eligible for entitlement programs contract, and the extra money in workers' pockets is spent and put right back into the economy. As retail sales increase, warehouse inventory needs restocking and production grows; sure enough, new hires are required to meet demand, profits increase, and dividend payouts go up. Who are the losers here?

However, when considering the causes and current state of middle-class purchasing power, the purchasing aspect of this phrase may be on life support, but the power is not. When GDP, corporate revenues, executive bonuses, shareholder payouts, stock prices, government spending, state and federal tax revenues, federal reserve monetary policy, inflation and value of the dollar, and treasury bond interest rates are all impacted mostly by the power of the consumer, there is in fact a way to break this 40-year-top-down, supply-side, laissez-faire, gilded-age-inequality, collective-bargaining-stripping, right-to-work-at-morally-wrong-wages cycle that has so mercilessly massacred the middle class. Consumers have the power to choose the products they purchase. Choosing an American-made product breaks one cycle and begins a new one in which simple market demand can return jobs back home, take workers off unemployment, and put them back on the job with a salary that contributes to state and federal taxes, social security, and the local economy. A local economy, dominated by small, family-owned businesses, once lined Main Street in Small Town, USA with storefronts containing actual stores, now reduced to just an isle in the big box. These were stores run by fellow consumers, not the giant corporation Walmart, whose annual revenue of $405 billion is equal to the size of the twenty-third largest GDP in the world, whose CEO Michael Duke earns $18.7 million a year, and whose owners' family wealth now exceeds the wealth of the bottom 40% of American families combined. And all of these massive profits come at a painful price: 85% of the products for sale on the shelves of Walmart are imports. When all of the profits go to the top, to a small elite minority, the majority does have the power to maintain its active role in the economy.

At the fundamental core of American Exceptionalism lies our long history of leading the free world in social responsibility; this is also the very reason why we are the richest, most powerful nation in the world. When we as a nation, as one, march together arm-in-arm and do not leave anyone behind, we are unstoppable. A quick snapshot of the progress, fairness, and equality that we have achieved in the twentieth century alone includes the 19th amendment allowing women the right to vote; the New Deal, otherwise known as the 3 R's: Relief for the poor, Recovery of a shattered economy, and Reform of broken financial system; and the Great Society with efforts to eliminate poverty and racial injustice and boost domestic discretionary spending on education, medical care, and infrastructure. Contrary to Milton Friedman's and Monetarist theories and the beliefs of Adam Smith, I believe that what makes us strong and serves as the main ingredient in our wealth as a nation is our obligation to take care of our own. Everyone who has the United States listed as their nationality should be held to the same standards and obligations of the social responsibility contract we call American Exceptionalism. And this includes American businesses. Much has changed since Adam Smith described the principles of what would eventually be known as capitalism, but one of the most significant factors is the evolution of the processes and practices involved with the production of goods and bringing these commodities to the market for trade, or—simply said—the deindustrialization of America. Because of an overriding focus on boosting shareholder value and meeting quarterly expectations, all has been abandoned in the name of dollar signs, including social responsibility and a moral obligation to the country in which business operates and to the workers who consume the goods that business provides. When Henry Ford doubled his workers' salaries to $5 a day in 1914, he wasn't thinking about EBITDA numbers or higher production costs eating away at short-term profits. No, what he imagined was a long-term investment in which the benefits would create a deeply rooted cycle of growth; when workers have enough money in their pockets, they in turn are able to buy the product you are selling.

And so here we are today, caught in a vicious cycle of deep structural economic stagnation in which the middle class has been laid on its back, as the powerful few and their sidekicks in Washington remain blind and oblivious to the storm ahead. We have lost sight of who we are, what we once were, and what has made us so great. If we do not change course now and prepare for a future global economic transformation, we as a nation will continue on a path of decline, with massive economic inequality, crumbling infrastructure, second-rate schools, continued investment abroad by large corporations, a workforce unprepared and unable to keep up with technological advances, and a retired baby-boom generation that no one can afford to take care of. Before we know it, American Exceptionalism and annual GDP growth above 2% will become a distant memory, as the American Dream evaporates.

The next time you find yourself lost in the labyrinth of seemingly endless isles of cereal, socks, and flat screen televisions, pushing a cart filled with items to purchase, take a minute to ask yourself: do you want a better life for your children than you have had? Do you want our country to prosper and continue to be a world leader? Do you want to know that you will be taken care of when you grow old? Then I ask you to look for that red, white, and blue "Made In America" tag. The future of our nation rests solely on whether or not we are able to look at ourselves in the mirror, accept the truth of what we have become as a nation and, most importantly, take responsibility for the actions and consequences of our past decisions. At this make-or-break moment in our nation's history, our future will be determined when we have the strength and courage to truly look at that reflection staring back at us. A country is not a company, and individual, short-term, short-sighted profits will never lead to the rewards of a long-term investment in which everyone reaps the benefits.

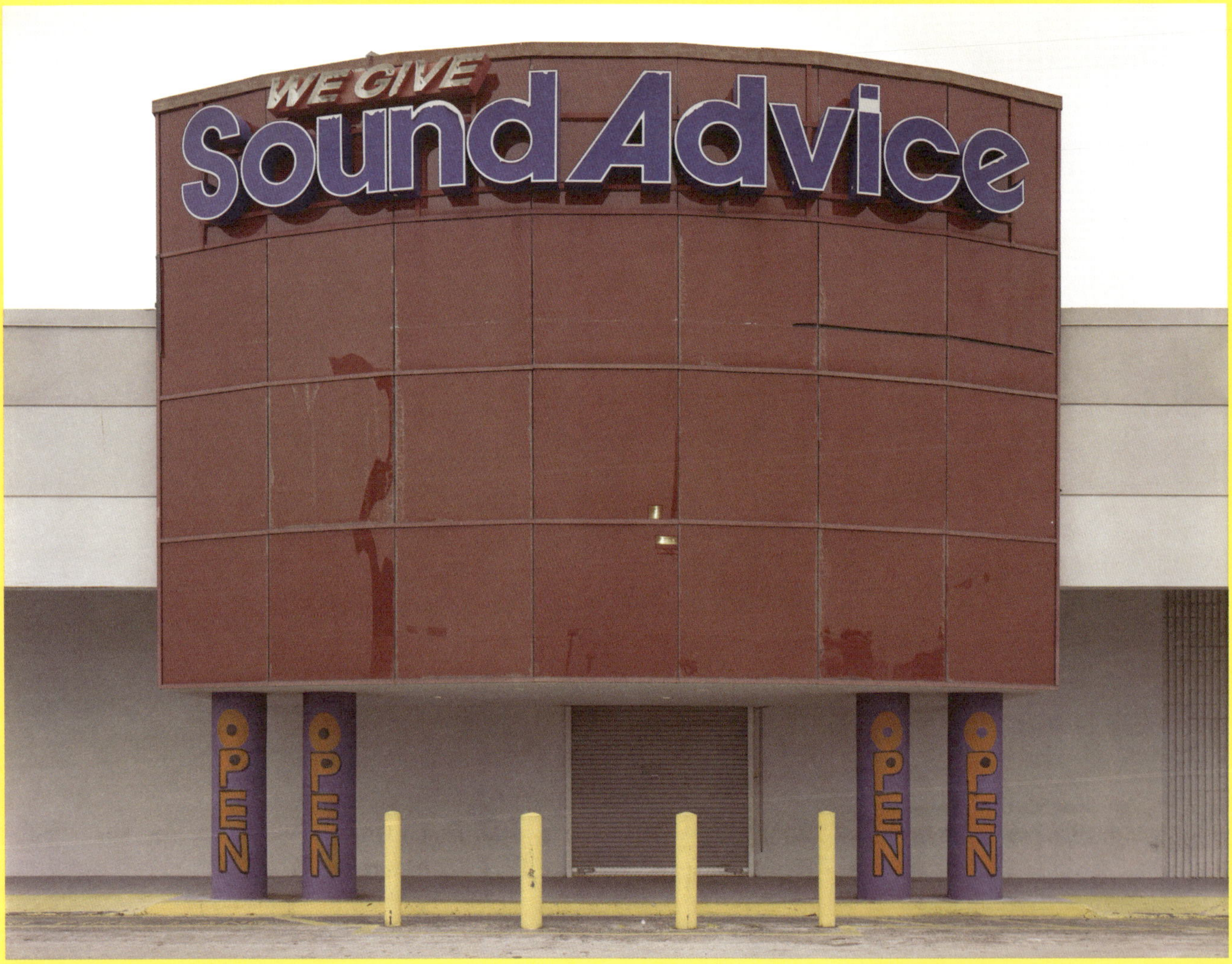

Brian Ulrich, *Sound Advice*, 2009
From the series *Dark Stores, Ghostboxes & Dead Malls*

Will Steacy (born 1980) is an American photographer and writer based in New York City. He comes from five generations of newspaper men and worked as a union laborer before becoming a photographer.

There's going to be a transfer of power, retail action and many other types of action from the central city to the southeast part of Cleveland. And we're not making statements today to discredit downtown. However, I believe that after today, the forces that want to keep downtown Cleveland intact had better get on their horse and start riding real fast.

Edward J. DeBartolo, Sr., 1976
Known as the father of the American shopping mall

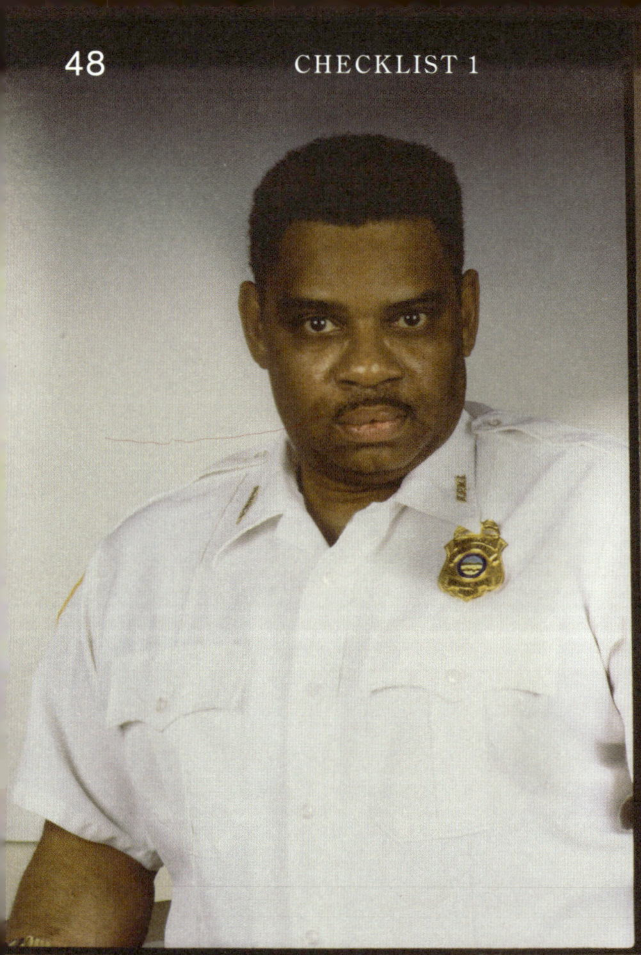

Account Summary
Division of Water

ACCOUNT NUMBER	METER NUMBER	READ DATE	CURRENT METER READ
59377514001-2		01/08/09	25670.4
SERVICE ADDRESS	TYPE OF READING	READ DATE	PREVIOUS METER READ
RANDALL PARK MALL LLC. WARRENSVILLE CTR RD NORTH RANDALL OH 44128	ACTUAL	10/07/08	25574.8
		BILLING DATE	CONSUMPTION 1000 CU FT
		01/08/09	95.6

PREVIOUS BALANCE $34,896.07

WATER CHARGE $4,127.64
CUSTOMER SERVICE CHARGE $7.00

AMOUNT DUE BY 01/27/09 $39,030.71

DIXIE SQUARE SHOPPING CENTER

PAYROLL SHEET

PAY PERIOD ENDING: 5-11-73

	NAME:	RT	OT	T.C.	REMARKS
1.	ALEXANDER, NATHAN	36	00	x	
2.	BAKER, MARSHALL	46	00	x	
3.	BOND, FRANK	41	00	x	RAISE DUE AS OF 4-8-73 3.00+15 = $3.15
4.	CLEMONS, RICHARD	13	00	x	
5.	CHILDS, THOMAS	40	00	x	
6.	DAVIS, WILLIAM	13	00	x	
7.	GARDNER, FLOYD	62	00	x	
8.	HODGE, WILLIAM	72	00	x	
9.	JACKSON, AUSTON V.	57½	00	x	9 hrs. lot patrol pay 62¢ PER HR.
10.	JACKSON, CARL	45½	00	x	
11.	SMITH, WALTER	80	00	x	
12.	SNEED, NORMAN	33	00	x	RAISE DUE AS OF 4-8-73 $3.00+15 = $3.15
13.	SNIDER, PAUL	80	05½	x	4hrs A.D.T. 05-05-73 40 HRS LOT PATROL PAY AT 62¢ PER HR.
14.	TAYLOR, ROOSEVELT	OFF		x	→
15.	THOMAS, HOMER	44	00	x	
16.	WORMICK, JAMES	80	00	x	8 hrs. Lot pay AT 62¢ PER. HR
	TOTAL:	743	5½		
1.	BENEGAS, SAMUEL	80	00	x	
2.	BURTON, JAMES	72½	00	x	
3.	CANNON, KEVIN	39	00	x	STARTED VACATION MAY-7-1973
4.	IRVING, JAMES	63½	00	x	
5.	KING, STEVE	24	00	x	RAISE DUE AS OF MAY-8-73 3.00+15 = $3.15
6.	PRICE, JOE	28	00	x	
7.	SMITH, SR. JAMES F.	74	02	x	
8.	SMITH, JR. JAMES F.	33	00	x	
9.	SMITH, WILLIAM	56½	00	x	
	TOTAL:	469½	2		
1.	RUSSELL, SR. CHARLES D.				
2.	ZESZUTKO, FRANCIE	4			
3.	KNIGHT, ROSE	80			
	TOTAL:	84			
	P.M. Snider				
	SUBMITTED BY P.M.SNIDER				APP'D BY C.D.RUSSELL SR.

M. C. HIGGINS, M. D.
REG. NO. 1592
PHYSICIAN AND SURGEON
PHONE ED. 1-0298
15426 CENTER HARVEY, ILLINOIS
HOURS: 11 TO 12, 2 TO 4 AND EVES. 6:30 TO 8 WEEKDAYS THURSDAY 11 TO 12 SAT. 10 TO 12:30
EXCEPT TUESDAY EVENING

Don Put In file

FOR ____ DATE 9-23-70

R ADDRESS ____

Earl Simpson was in my office for treatment this afternoon.

M.C. Higgins M.D.

OLIVER Rexall DRUGS
COR. 154TH ST. AND CENTER AVE.
HARVEY, ILLINOIS
PHONE ED 3-3434

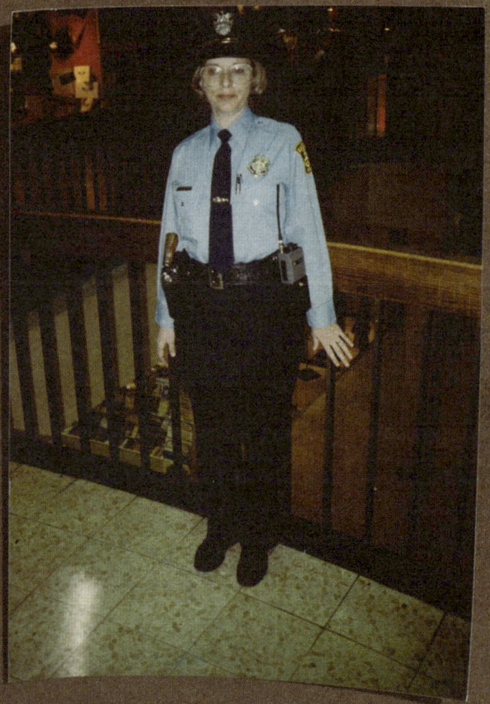

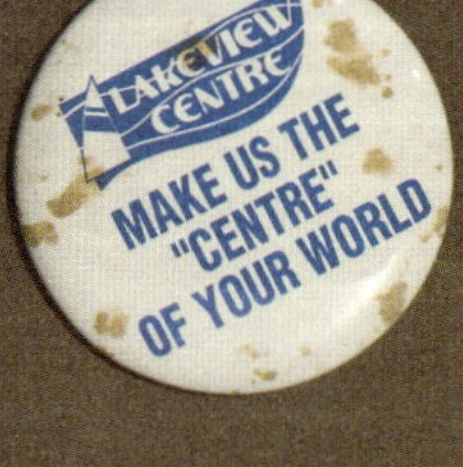

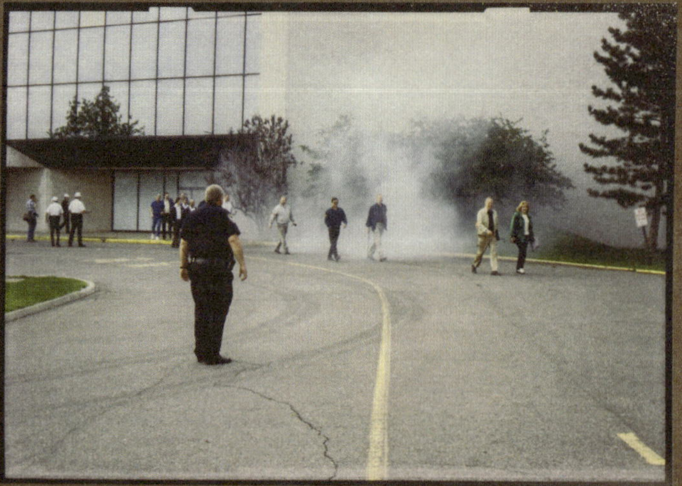

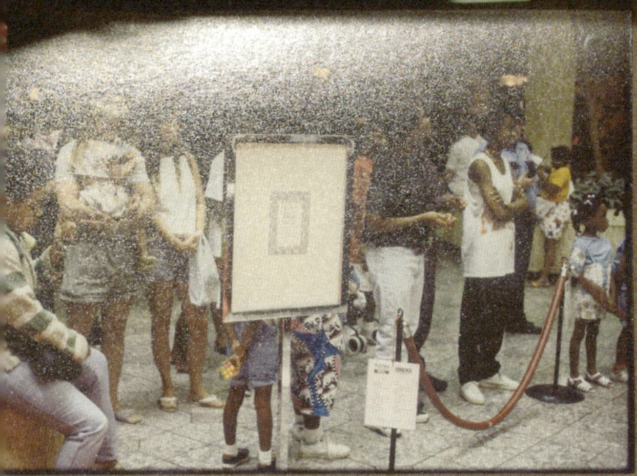

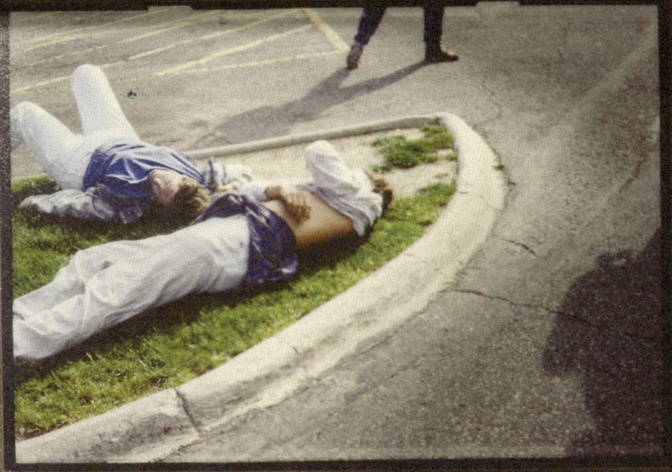

62

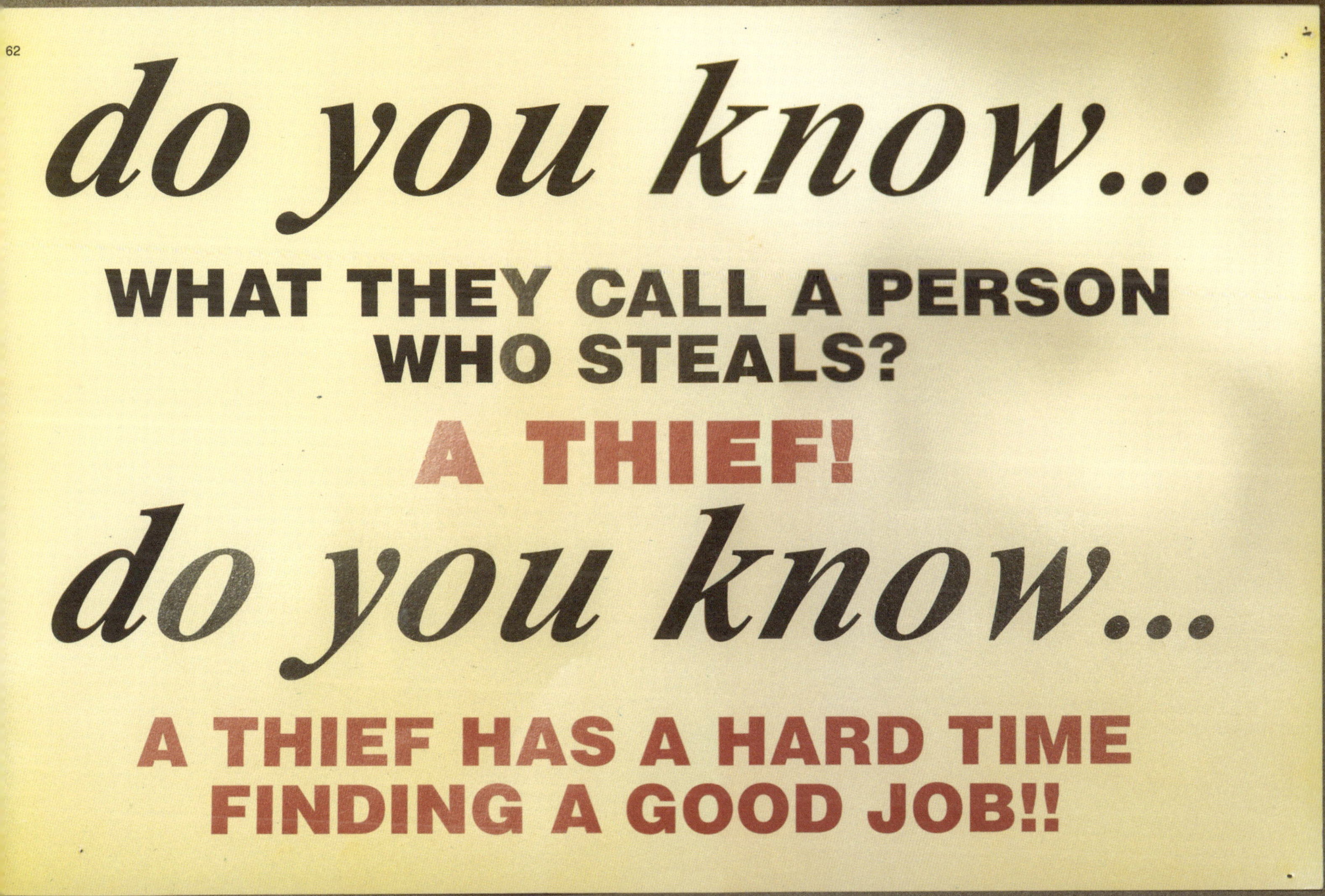
do you know...
WHAT THEY CALL A PERSON
WHO STEALS?
A THIEF!
do you know...
A THIEF HAS A HARD TIME
FINDING A GOOD JOB!!

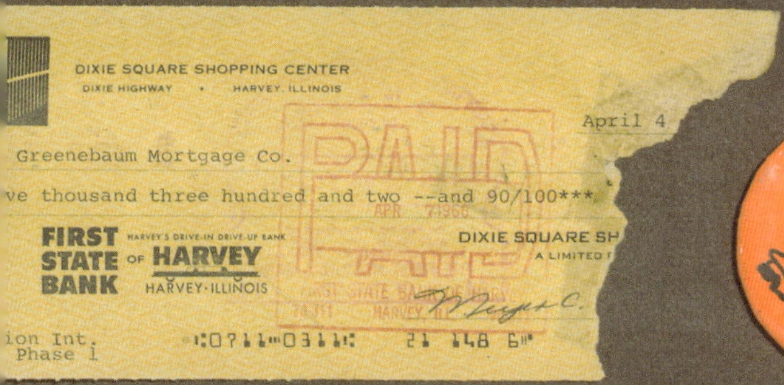
DIXIE SQUARE SHOPPING CENTER
DIXIE HIGHWAY • HARVEY, ILLINOIS
April 4
Greenebaum Mortgage Co.
ve thousand three hundred and two --and 90/100***
PAID
FIRST STATE BANK OF HARVEY
HARVEY·ILLINOIS
DIXIE SQUARE SH
ion Int.
Phase I

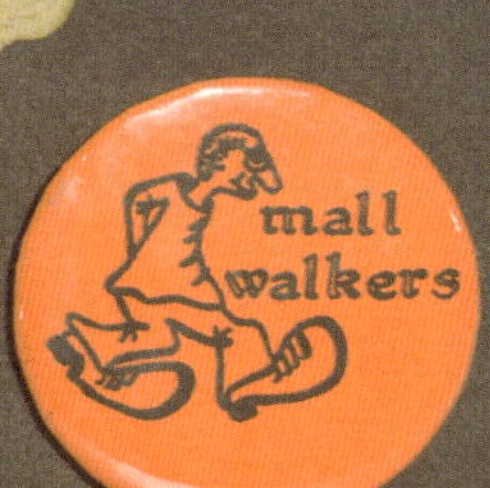
mall
walkers

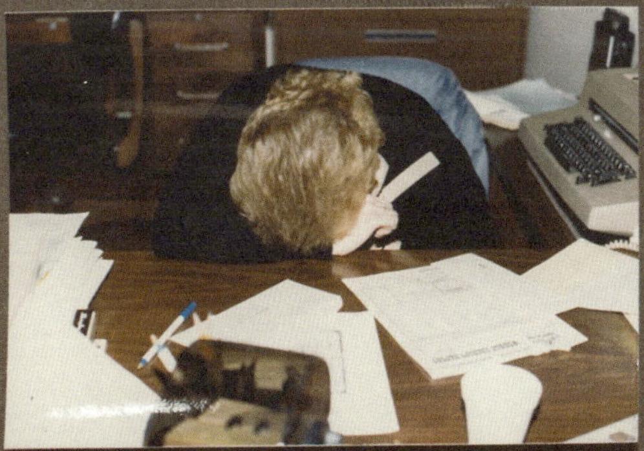

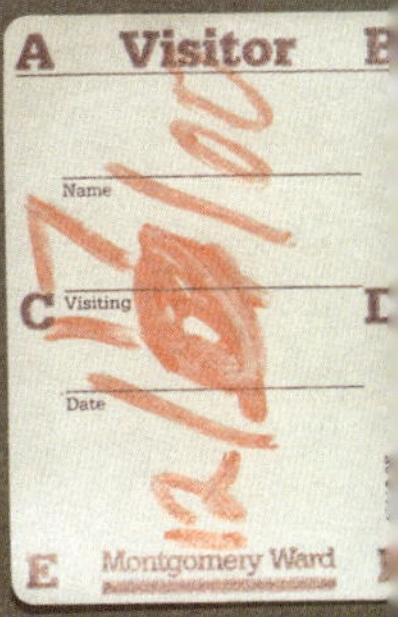
A Visitor B
Name
C Visiting D
Date
E Montgomery Ward

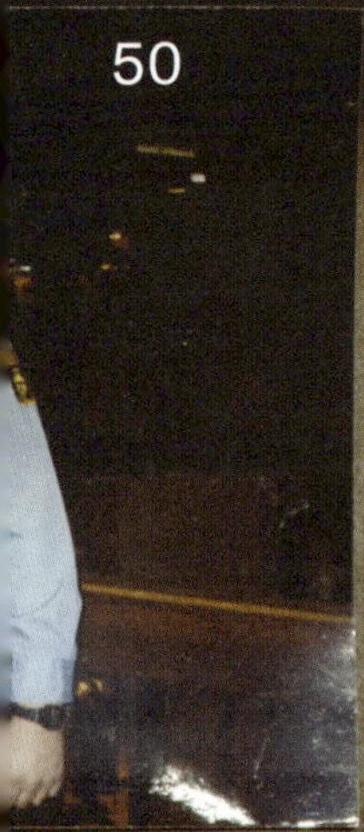

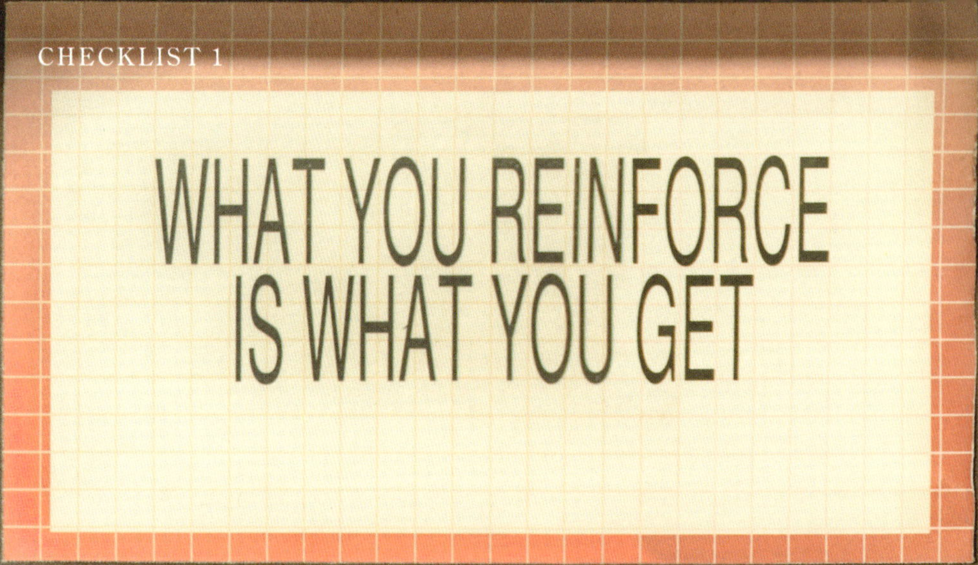

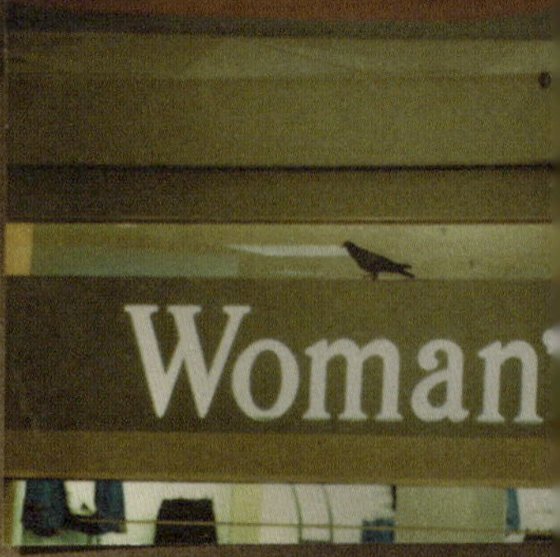

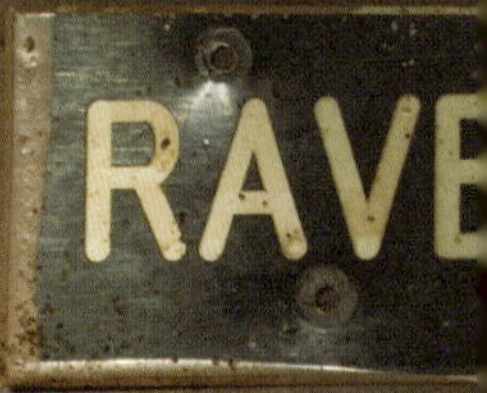

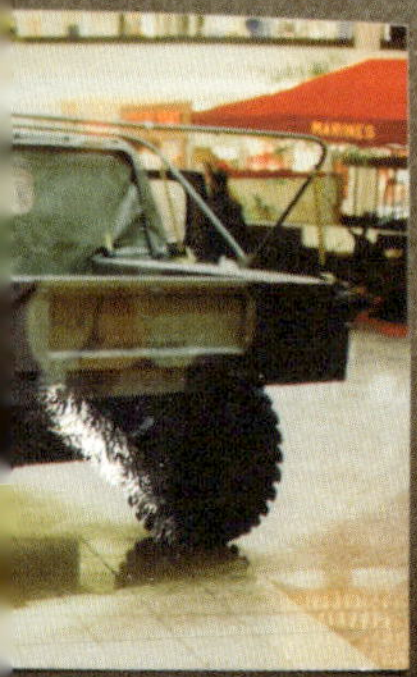

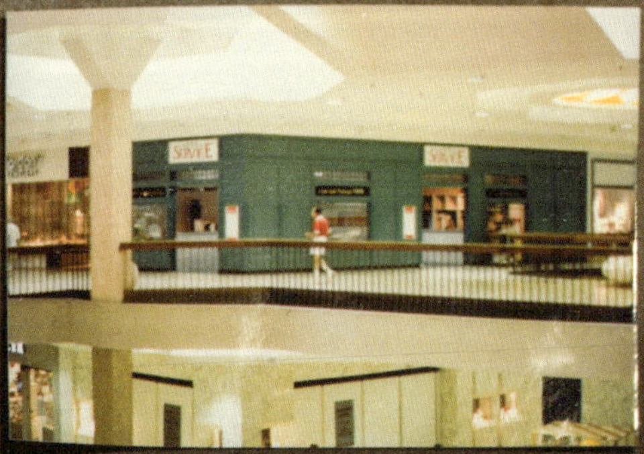

BOURBON STREET MALL
French Quarter
New Orleans, Louisiana

ALISS & CO:
WHATS UP? WELL I'M
HAVING A GRAND OL' TIME. SEEING
THE SIGHTS OF N.O. THIS IS
BOURBON ST. I FIGURED I'D
SHOW YALL WHERE I GOT
DRUNK AS A SKUNK (JUST TO
RUB IT IN) BUT ANYWAY I'LL
SEE YALL IN A FEW DAYS

POST CARD

ALYSSA CAPLAN
C/O G.H BASS &
110 FRONT ST. SU
WORC. COMM. FASH. ... TS
WORC. MASS. 01608

SPACE RESERVED FOR U.S. POSTAL SERVICE

2US LA 153
PB-16
John Hinde Curteich Inc. ©
Designed and Printed in the U.S.A.

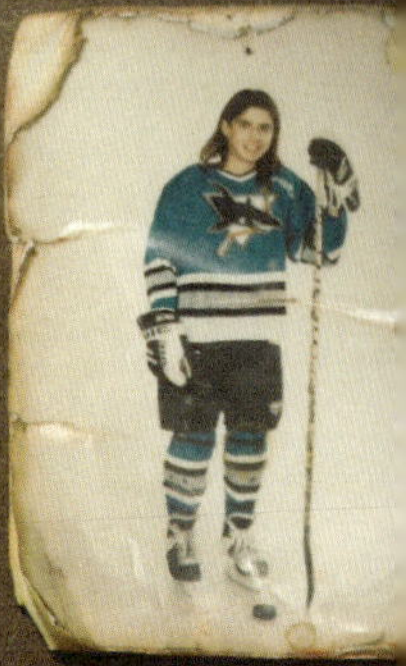

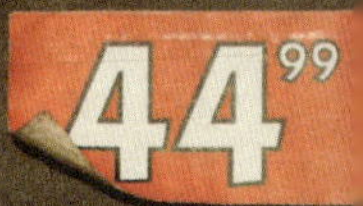

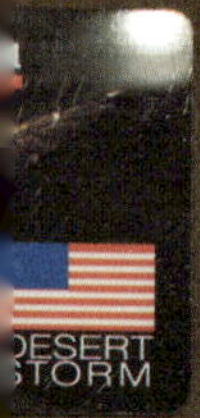

LL
ES, INC
RNPIKE
225

ER

ATION

BIT PARKING

ANE

HORNBACH-STEENWYK-THRALL, INC., ARCHITECTS
... AVENUE N.W. · GRAND RAPIDS MICHIGAN 49502 · TELEPHONE ...

REC'D
Initial | Date

November 15, 1965

Woolworth
Construction

DIXIE SQUARE SHOPPING CENTER
Dixie Highway
Harvey, Illinois

Attention: Mr. Sheldon Kantoff

SUBJECT: Woolworth's

Dear Shelly:

Your inability to arrange a meeting with Bill Thompson of Woolworth's is unfortunate.

The purpose of this letter is to "cover our tracks" should any further unreasonable accusations of delay be placed upon our shoulders.

Sincerely,

Don Steenwyk

DRS:bjd

WILLIAM F. THRALL — DONALD R. STEENWYK — CHARLES E. HORNBACH

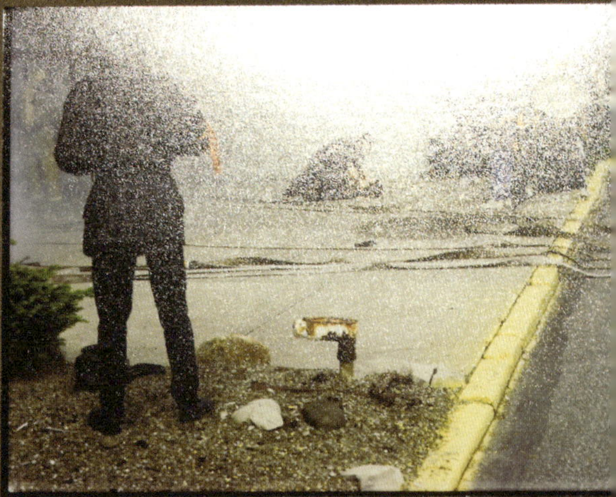

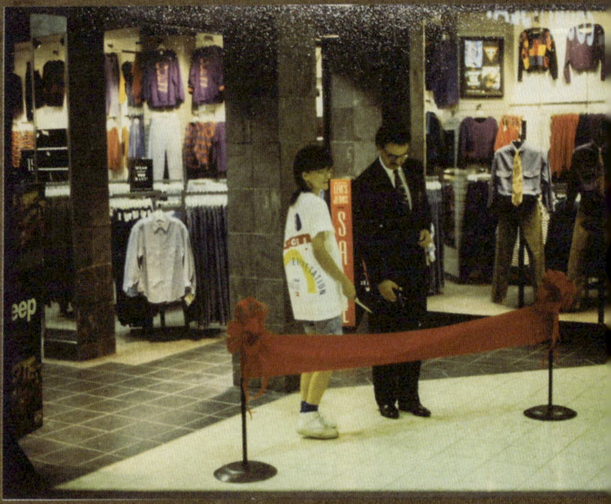

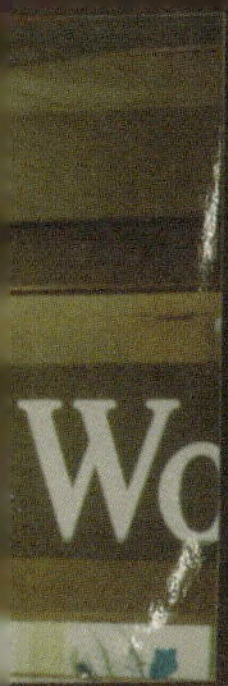

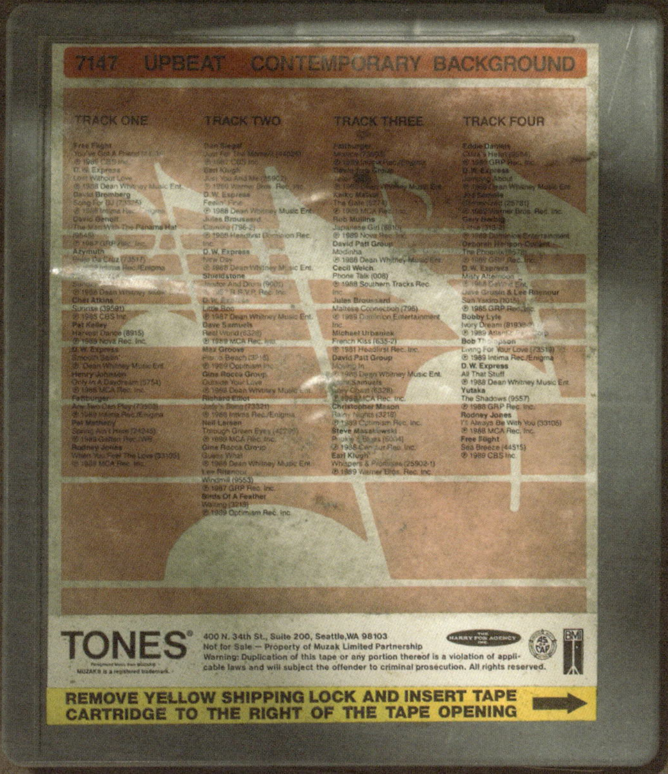

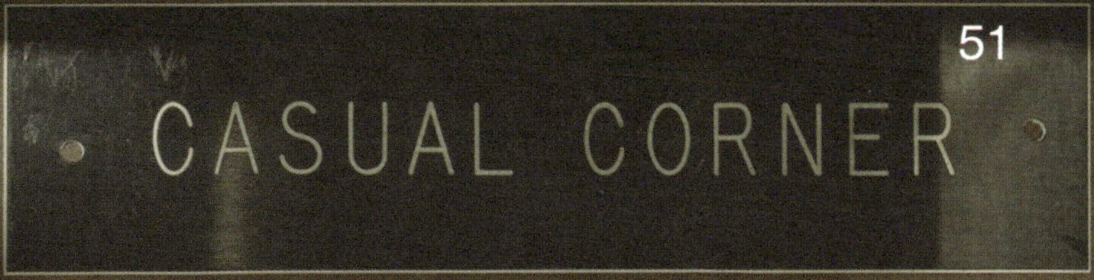

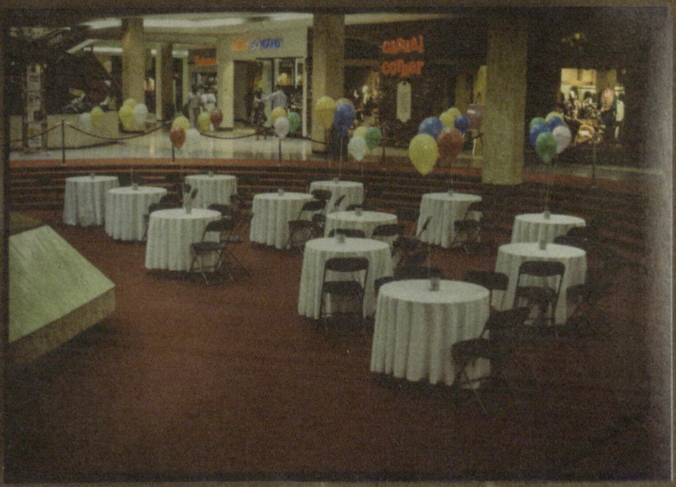

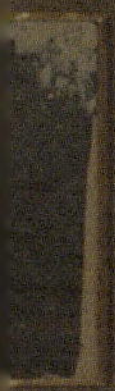

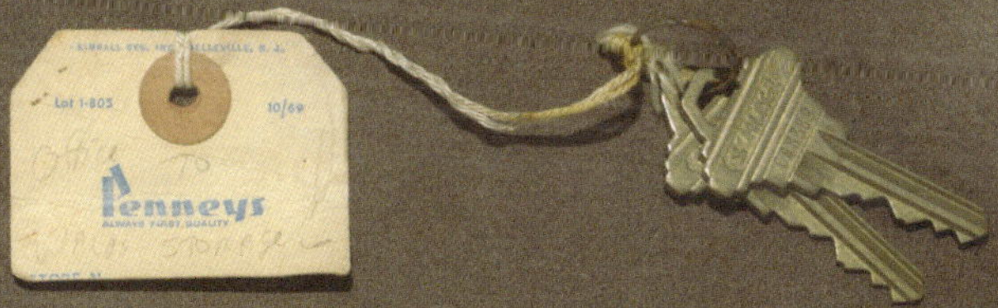

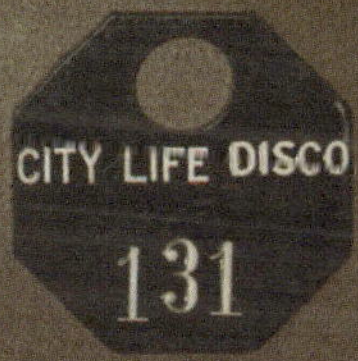

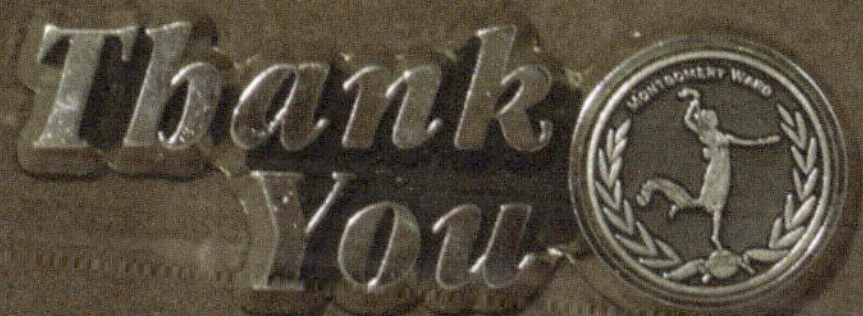

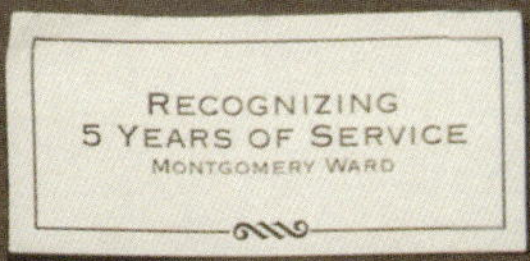

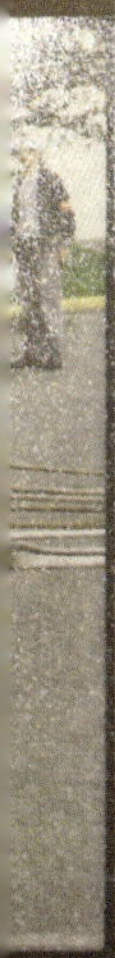

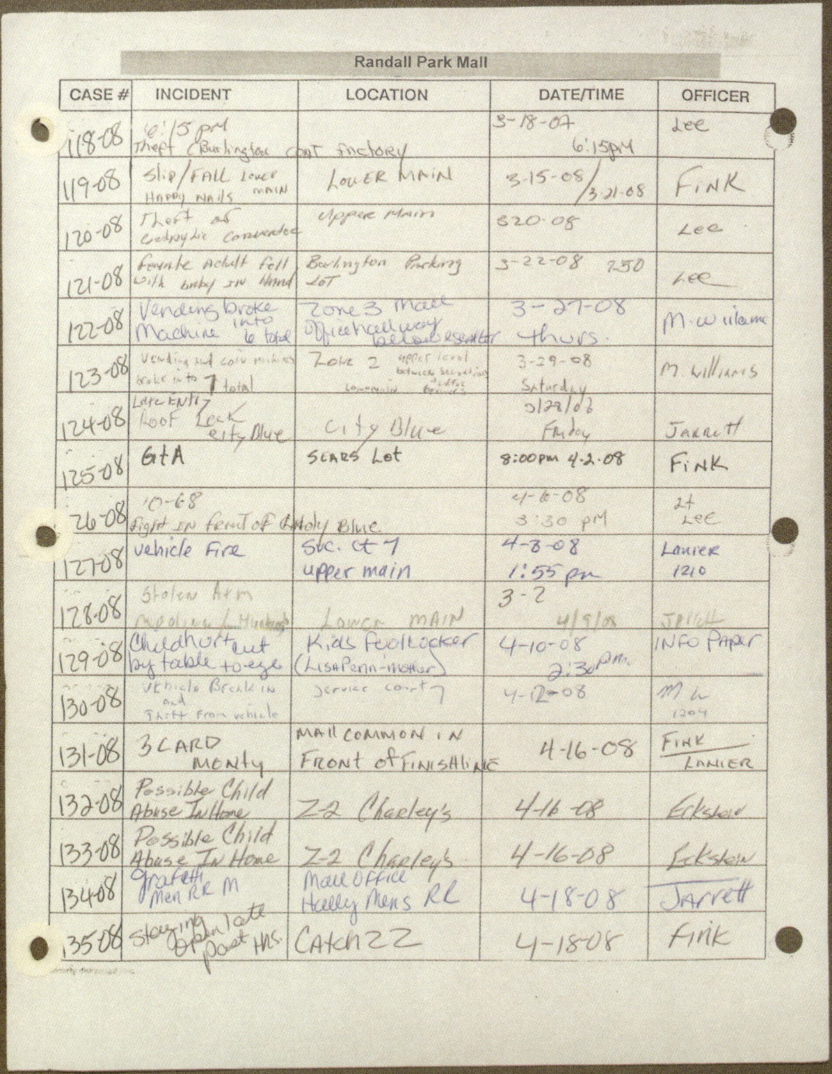

Randall Park Mall

CASE #	INCIDENT	LOCATION	DATE/TIME	OFFICER
118-08	6:15 pm Theft Burlington coat factory		3-18-07 6:15pm	Lee
119-08	Slip/Fall Lower main Happy Nails	Lower Main	3-15-08/3-21-08	Fink
120-08	Theft of catalytic converter	Upper Main	3-20-08	Lee
121-08	Female adult fell with baby in hand	Burlington Parking Lot	3-22-08 2:50	Lee
122-08	Vending Machine broke into 6 total	Zone 3 Mall Office hallway below escalator	3-27-08 thurs.	M. Williams
123-08	Vending and coin machines broke into 7 total	Zone 2 upper level between escalators lower main	3-29-08 Saturday	M. Williams
124-08	Larceny Roof Leak City Blue	City Blue	3/28/08 Friday	Jarrett
125-08	GTA	Sears Lot	8:00pm 4-2-08	Fink
126-08	10-68 fight in front of Holy Blue		4-6-08 3:30 pM	Lt Lee
127-08	vehicle Fire	Svc. Ct 7 upper main	4-8-08 1:55 pm	Lanier 1210
128-08	Stolen Arm	Lower MAIN	3-2 4/9/08	
129-08	Child hurt cut by table to eye	Kids Footlocker (Lisa Penn-mother)	4-10-08 2:30 pm	INFO Paper
130-08	Vehicle Break in and Theft from vehicle	Service court 7	4-12-08	M W 1204
131-08	3 CARD MONTY	MALL COMMON IN FRONT of FINISH LINE	4-16-08	Fink Lanier
132-08	Possible Child Abuse In Home	Z-2 Charley's	4-16-08	Eckstein
133-08	Possible Child Abuse In Home	Z-2 Charley's	4-16-08	Eckstein
134-08	grafetti Men RR M	Mall Office Holly Mens RR	4-18-08	Jarrett
135-08	Staying open late past HRS.	Catch 22	4-18-08	Fink

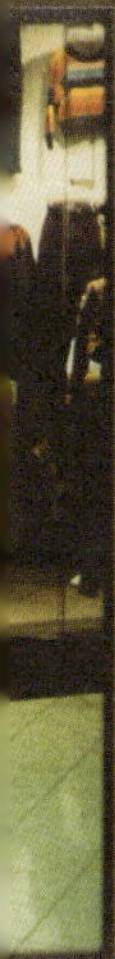

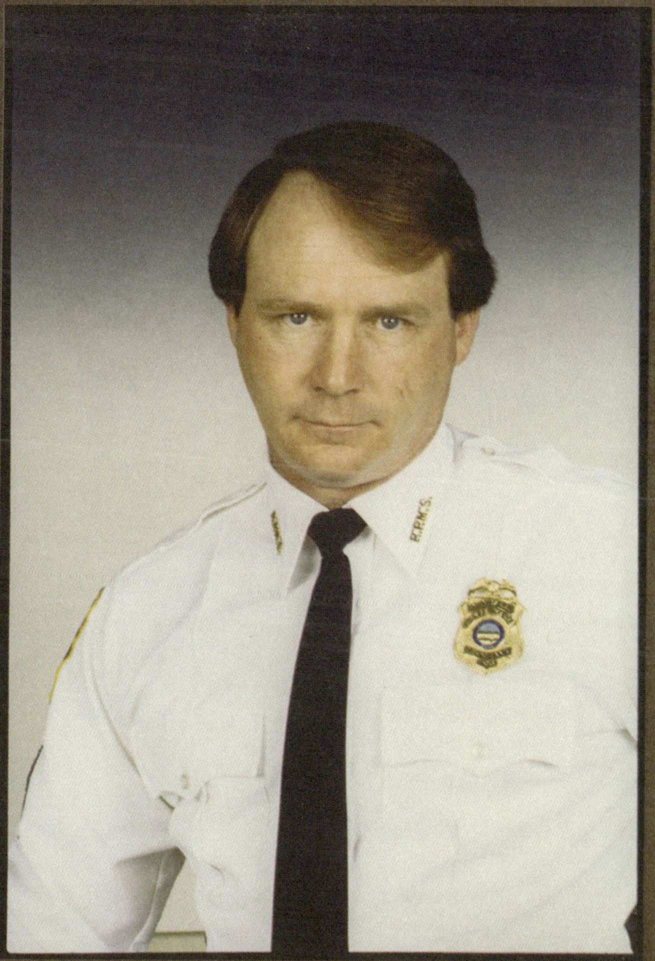

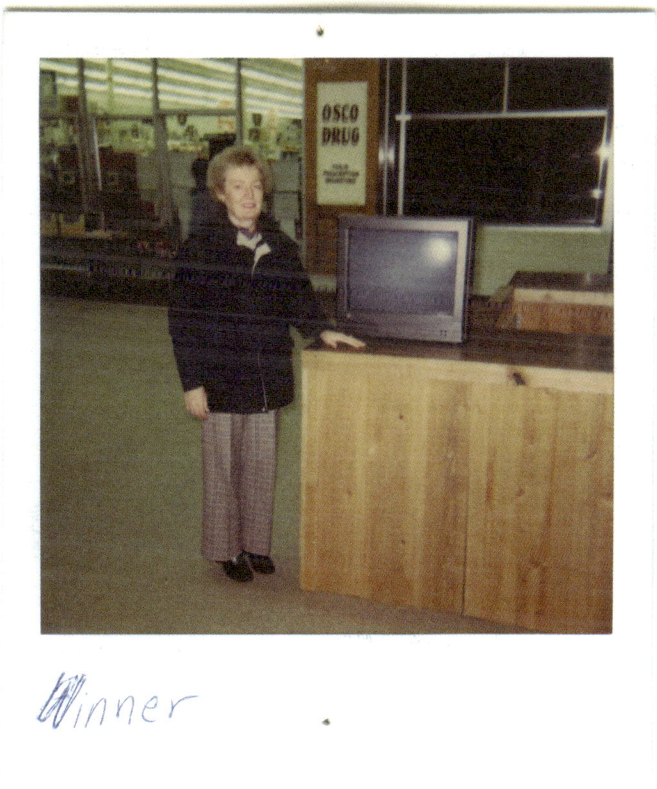
OSCO
DRUG
Winner

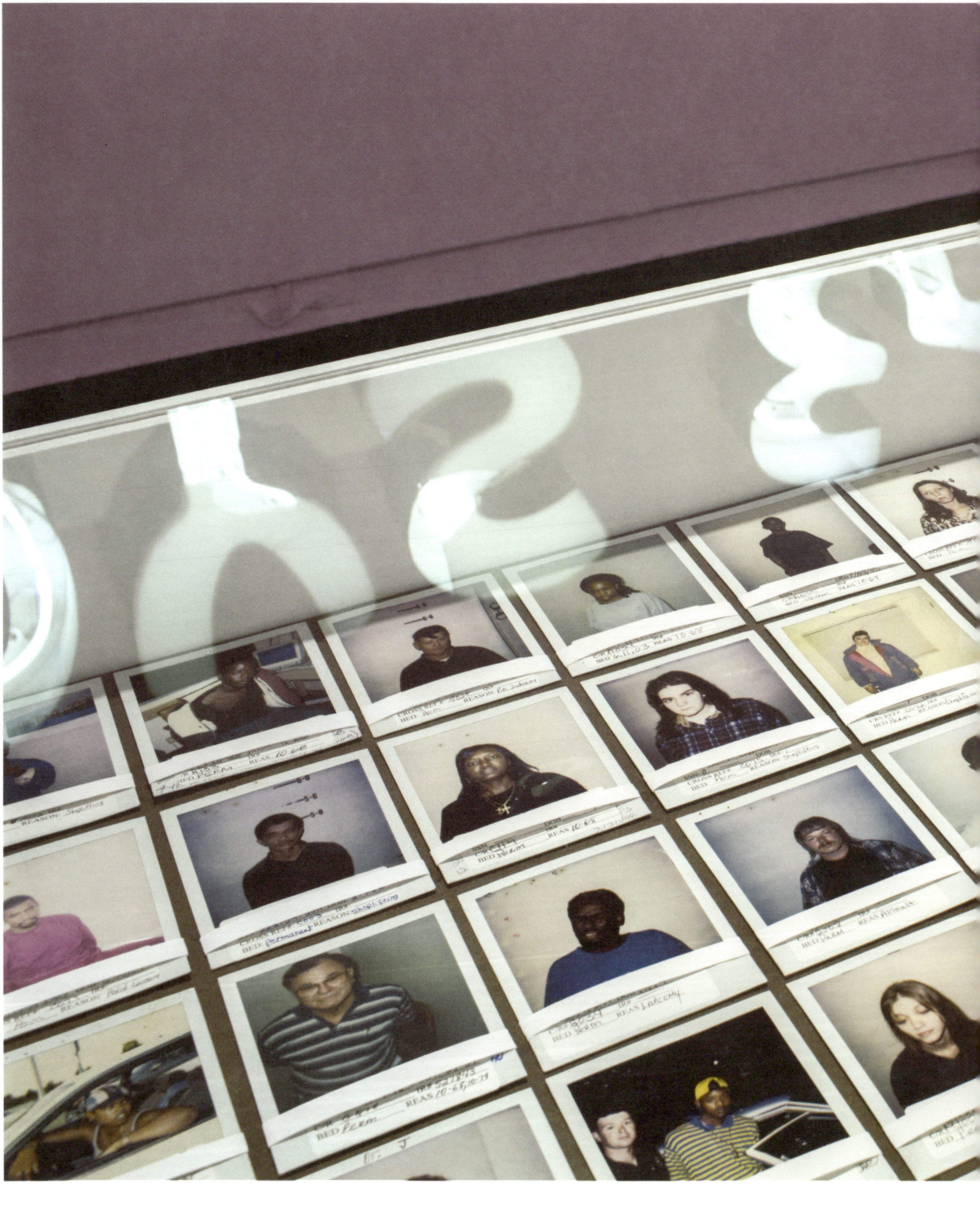

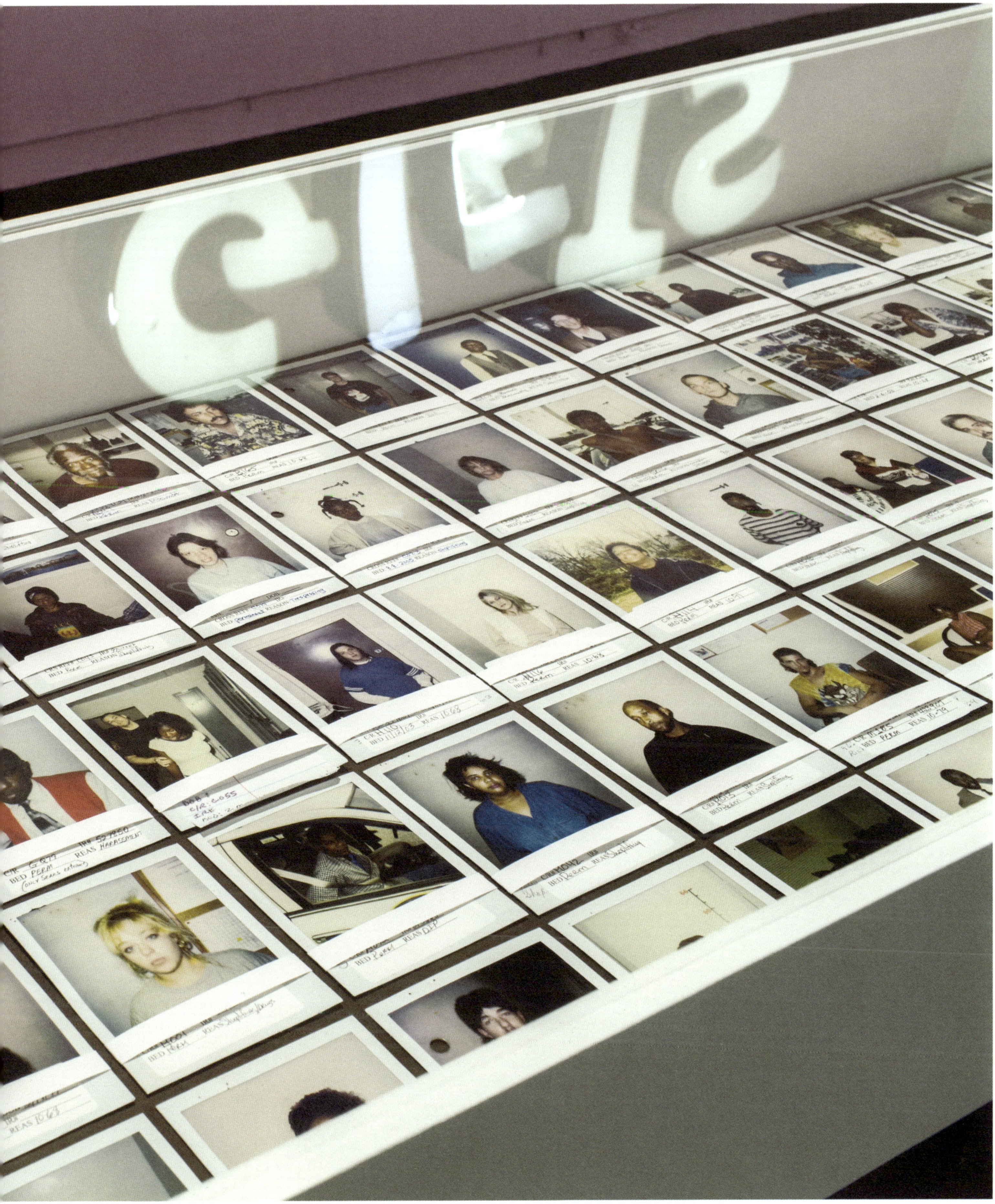

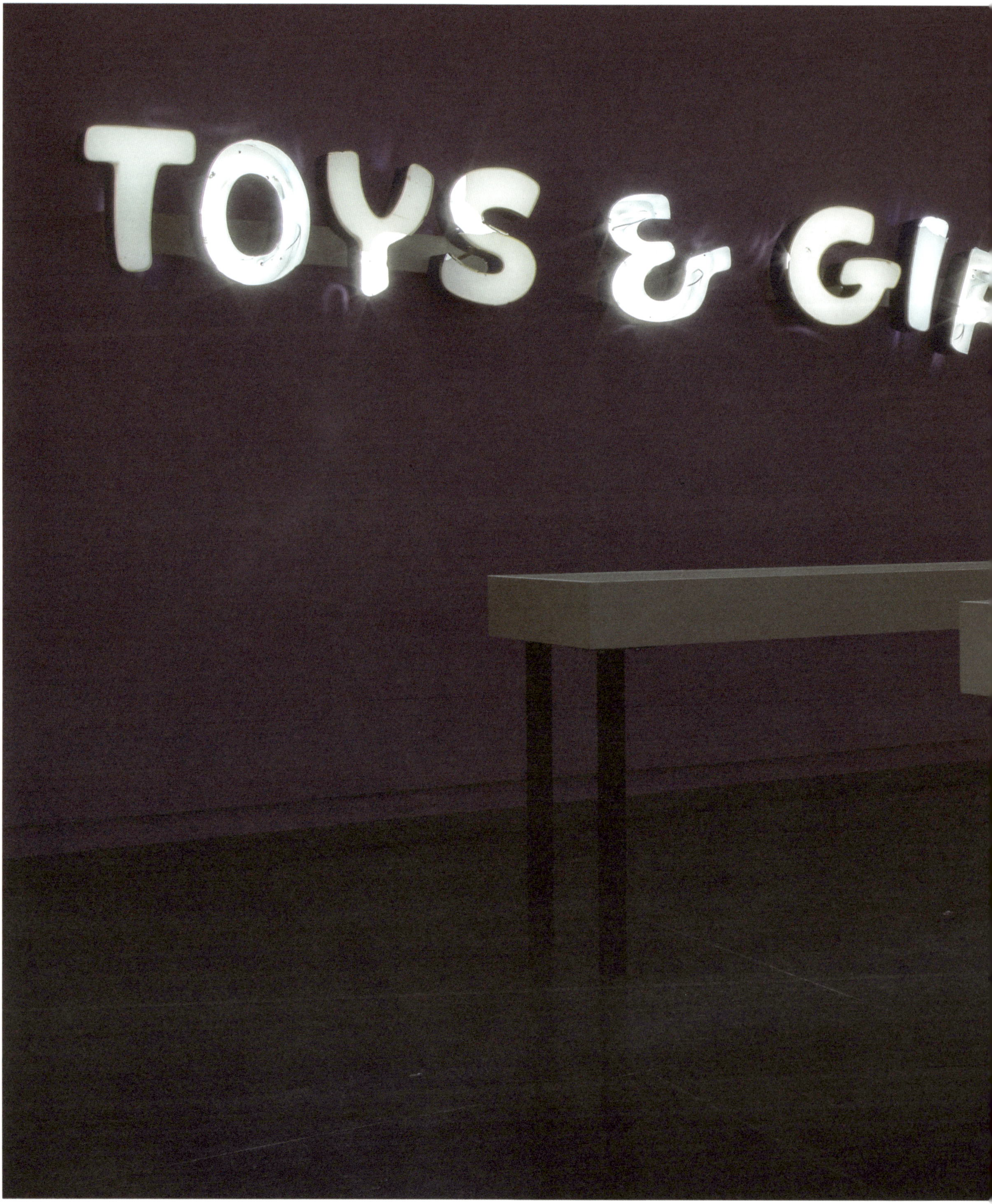
TOYS & GI

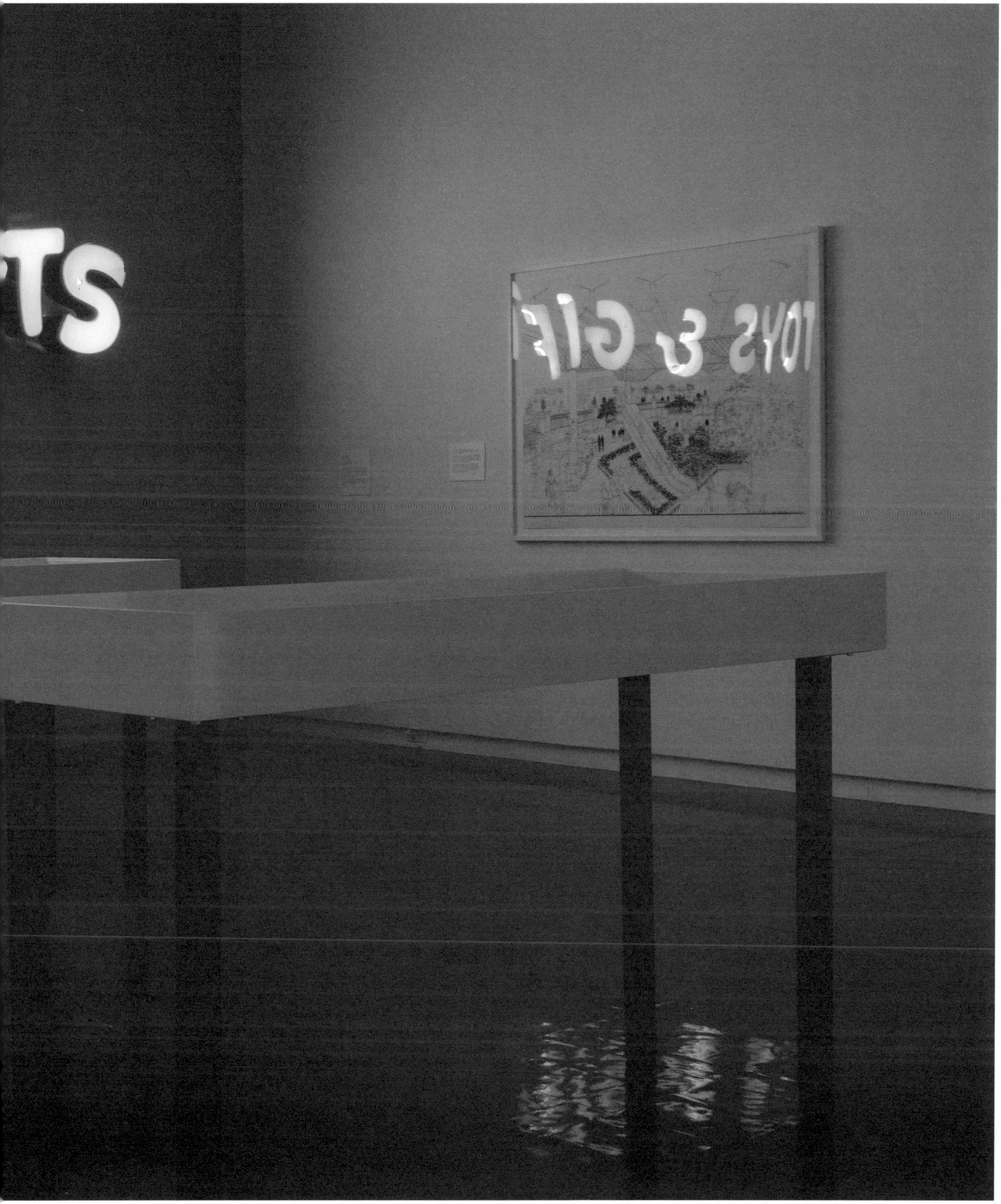

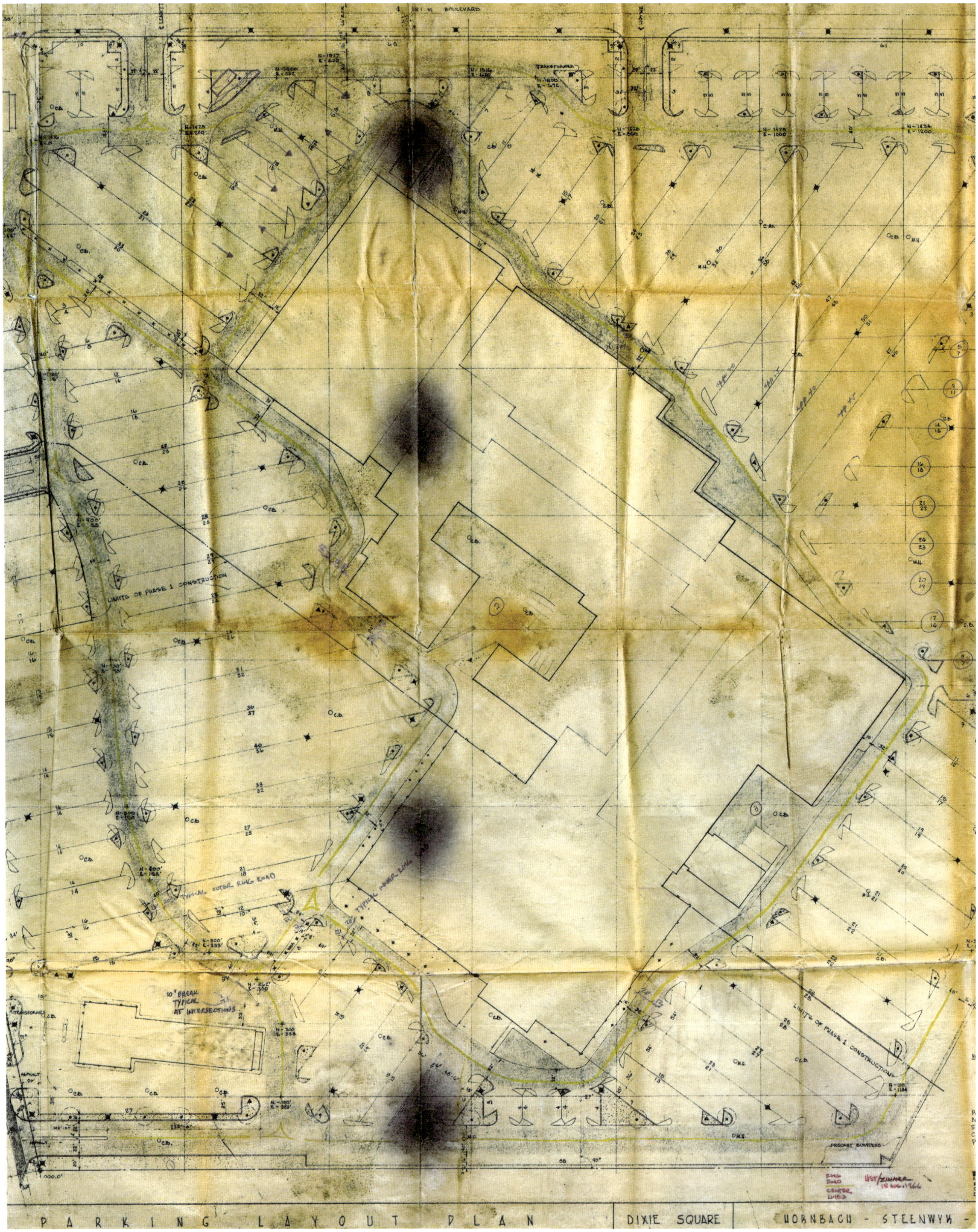
LIMITS OF PHASE 1 CONSTRUCTION
TYPICAL OUTER RING ROAD
10' BREAK TYPICAL AT INTERSECTIONS
LIMITS OF PHASE 1 CONSTRUCTION
PRECAST BUMPERS
PARKING LAYOUT PLAN
DIXIE SQUARE
HORNBACH - STEENWYK -

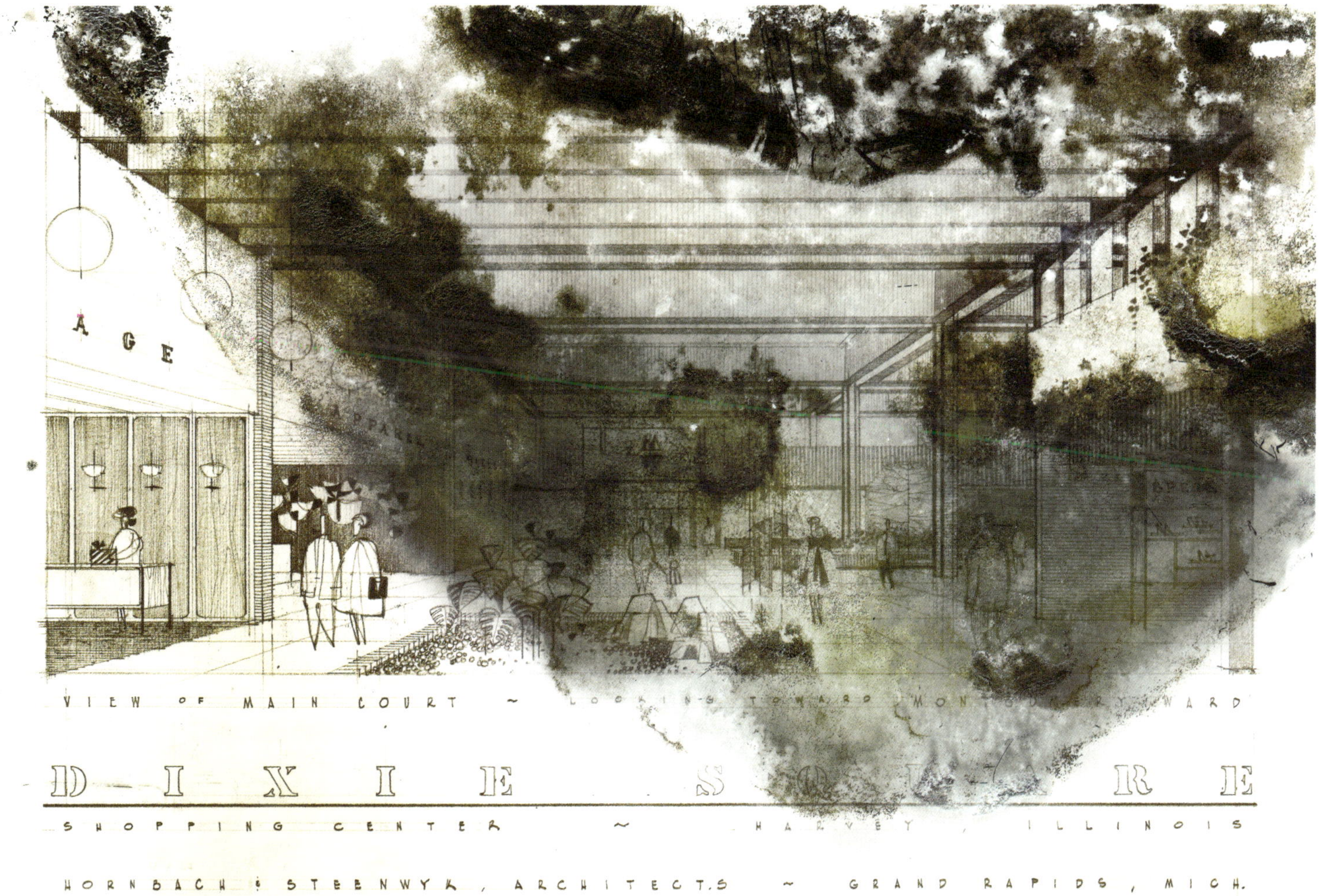
VIEW OF MAIN COURT ~
SHOPPING CENTER ~ HARVEY, ILLINOIS
HORNBACH & STEENWYK, ARCHITECTS ~ GRAND RAPIDS, MICH.

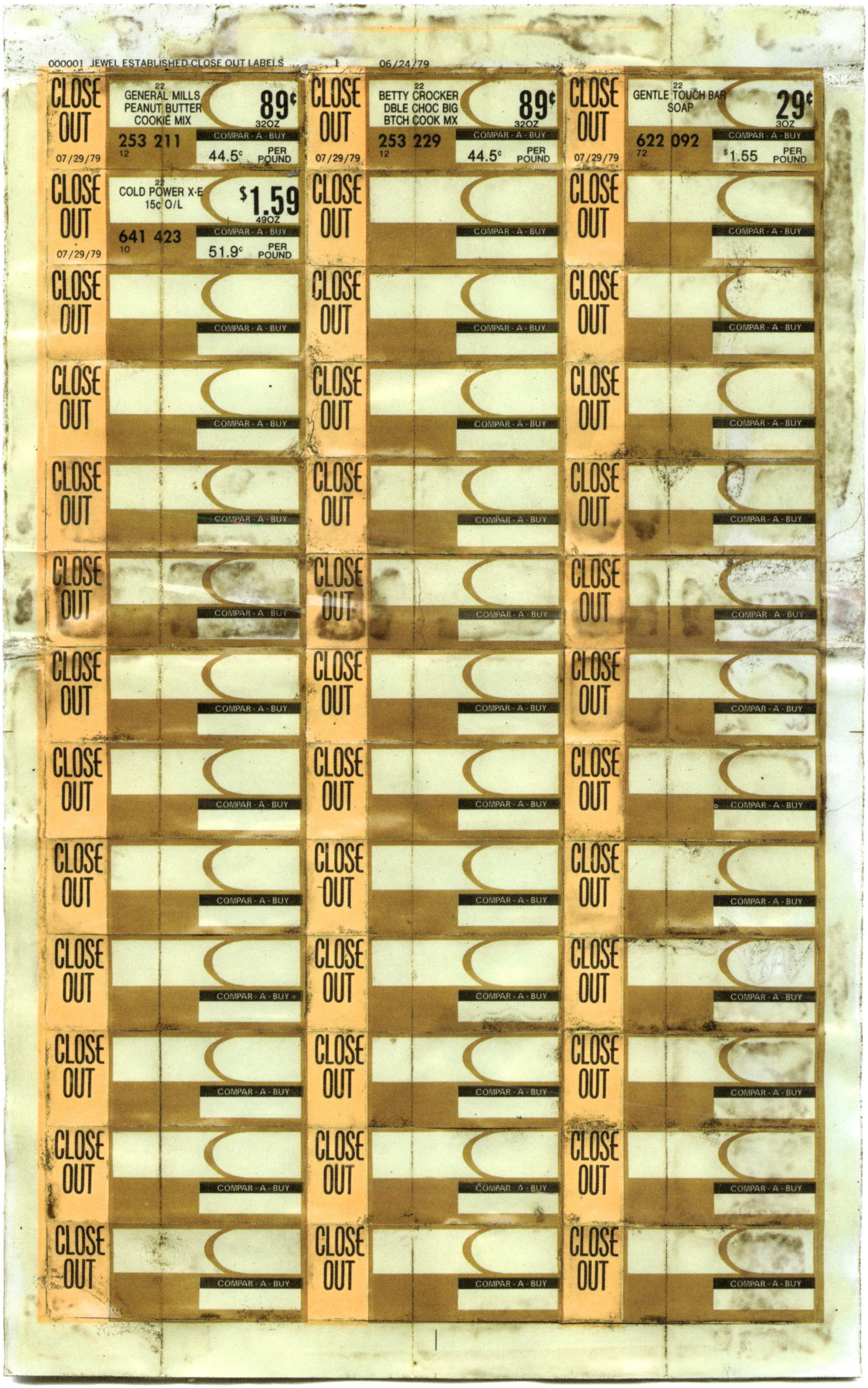
000001 JEWEL ESTABLISHED CLOSE OUT LABELS 1 06/24/79
CLOSE OUT 07/29/79
22 GENERAL MILLS PEANUT BUTTER COOKIE MIX
89¢ 32OZ
253 211 12
COMPAR-A-BUY
44.5¢ PER POUND
CLOSE OUT 07/29/79
22 BETTY CROCKER DBLE CHOC BIG BTCH COOK MX
89¢ 32OZ
253 229 12
COMPAR-A-BUY
44.5¢ PER POUND
CLOSE OUT 07/29/79
22 GENTLE TOUCH BAR SOAP
29¢ 3OZ
622 092 72
COMPAR-A-BUY
$1.55 PER POUND
CLOSE OUT 07/29/79
22 COLD POWER X-E 15c O/L
$1.59 49OZ
641 423 10
COMPAR-A-BUY
51.9¢ PER POUND

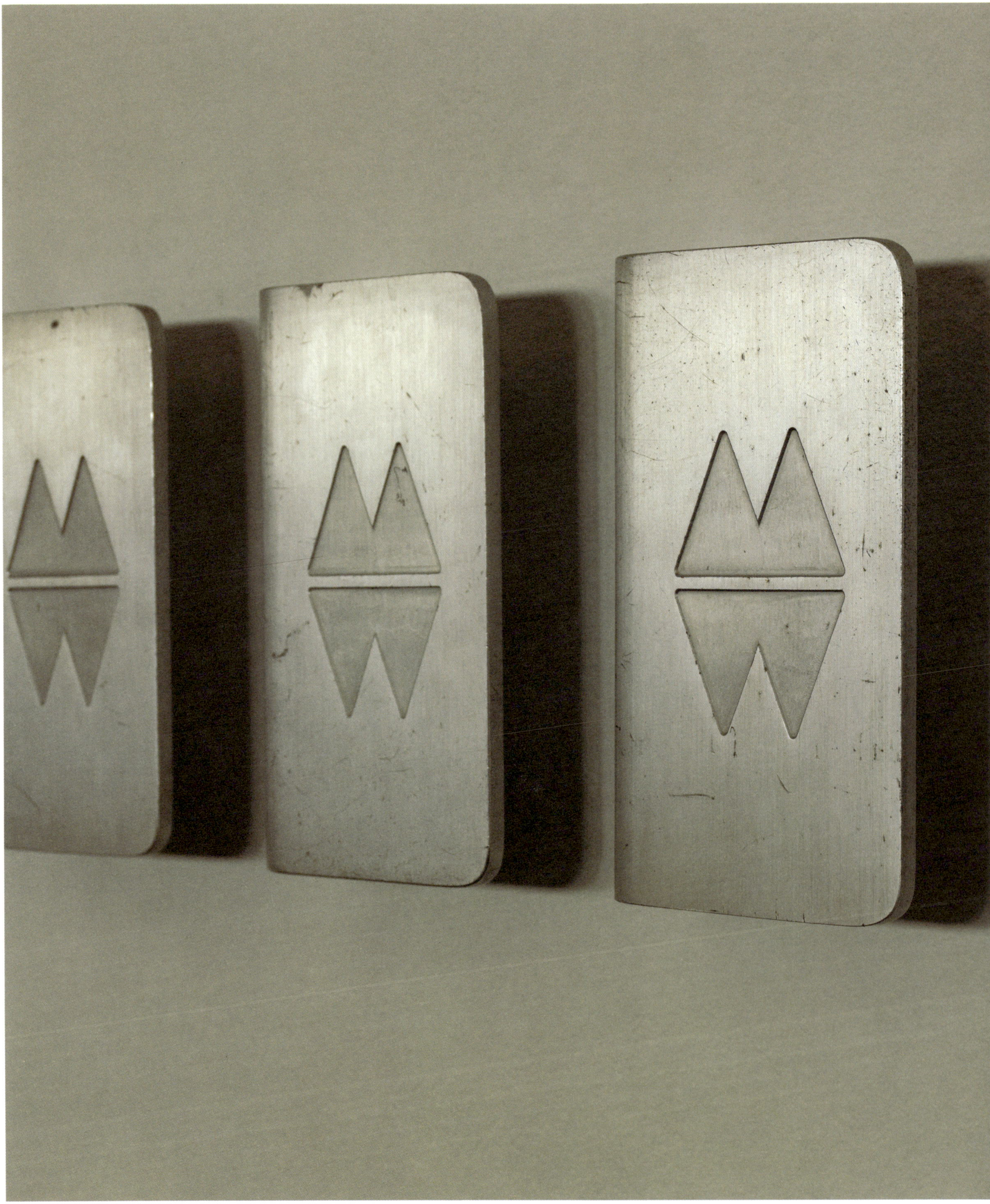

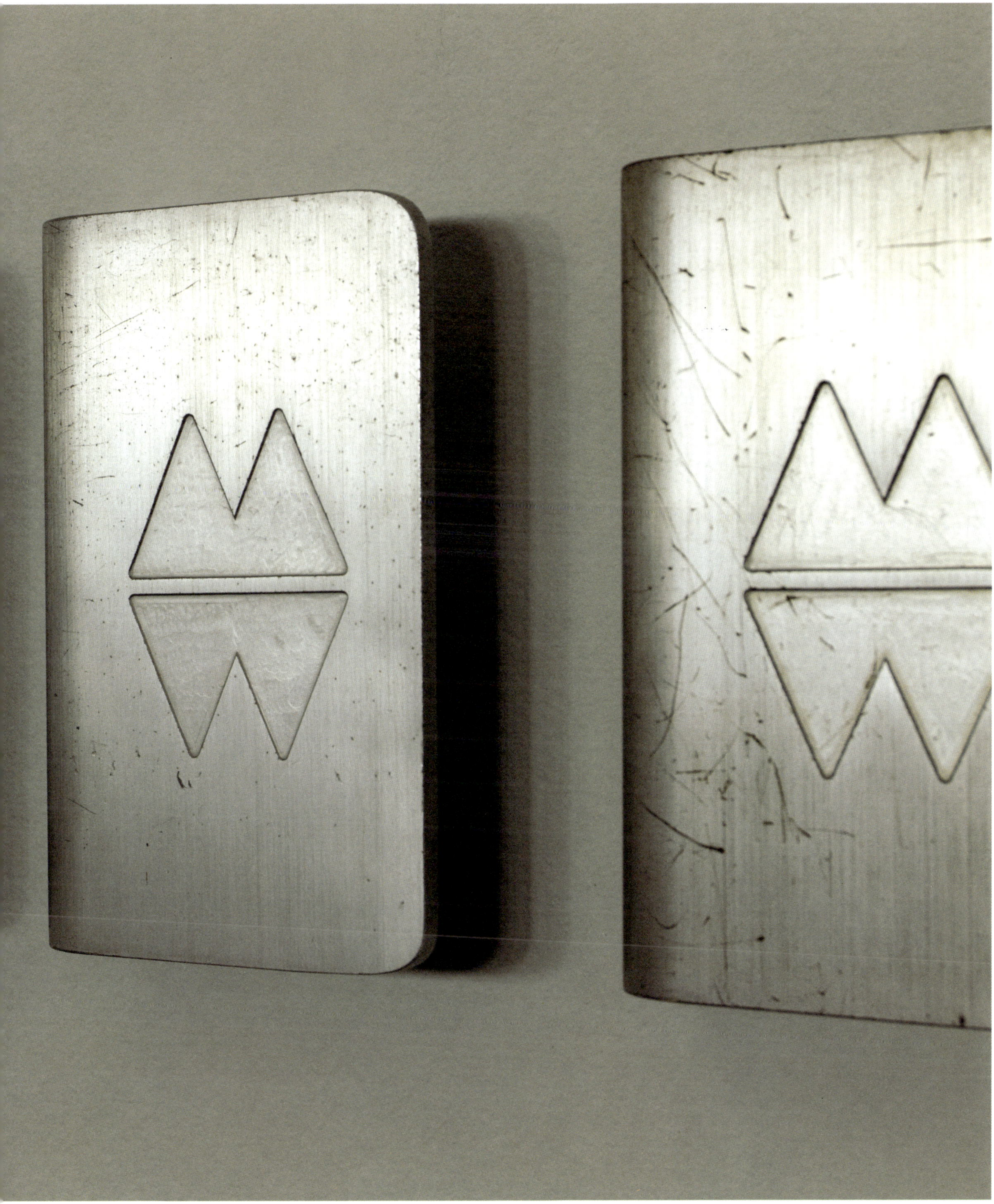

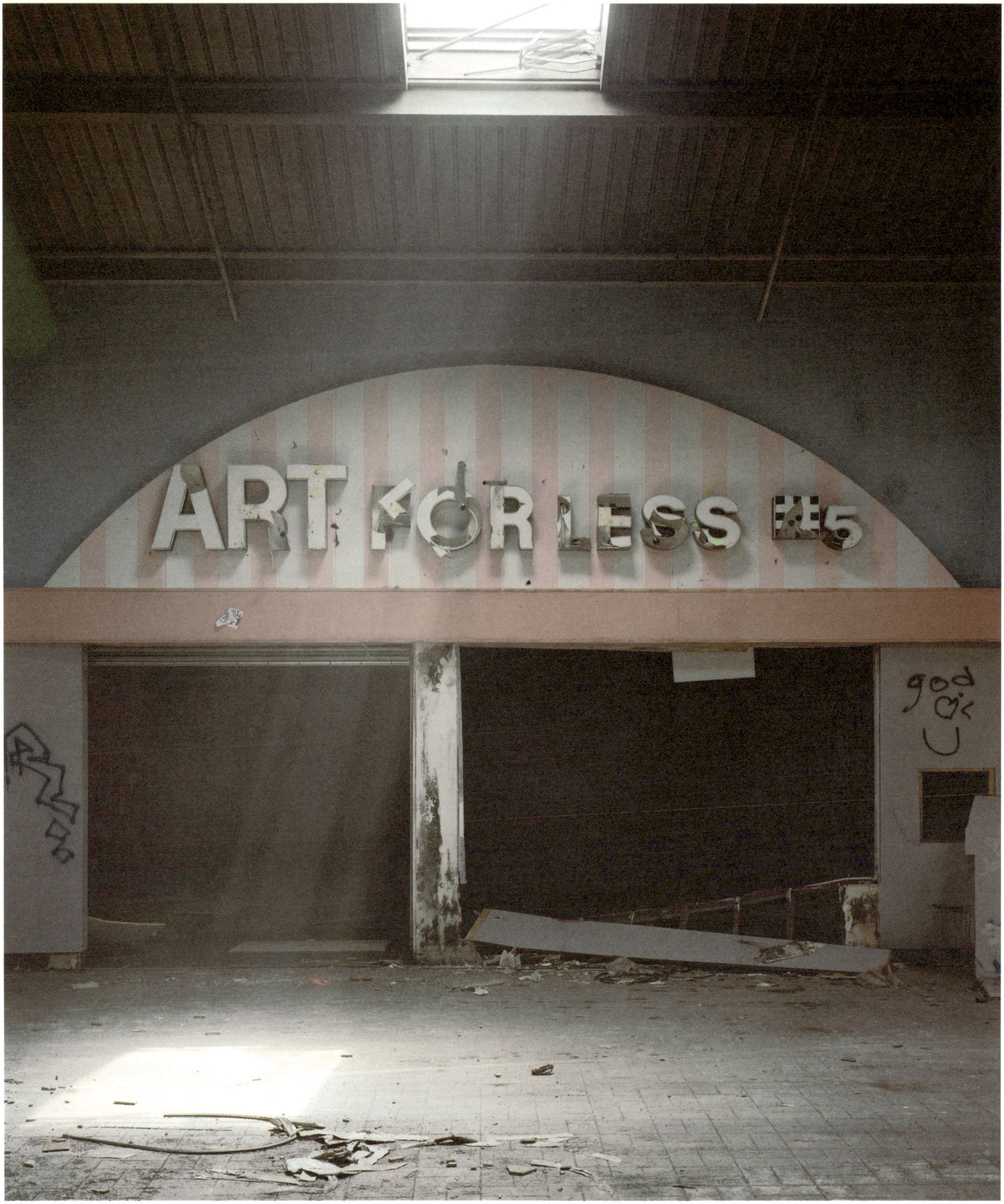

Brian Ulrich, *Art for Less #5,* 2009
From the series *Dark Stores,*
Ghostboxes & Dead Malls

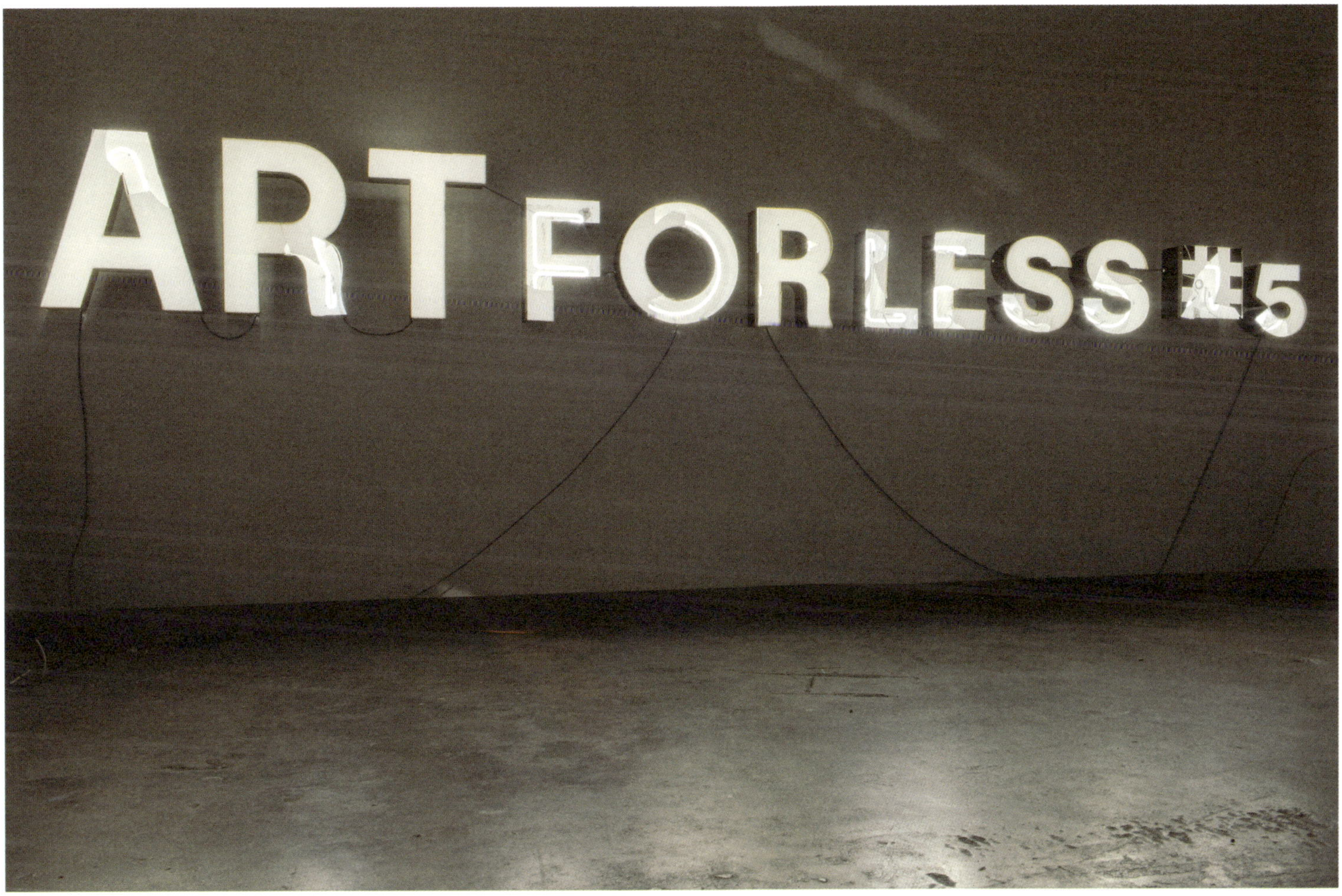
ART FOR LESS #5

dynakit STEREO 70
DYNAKIT STEREO 70
DYNA STEREO PREAMPLIFIER

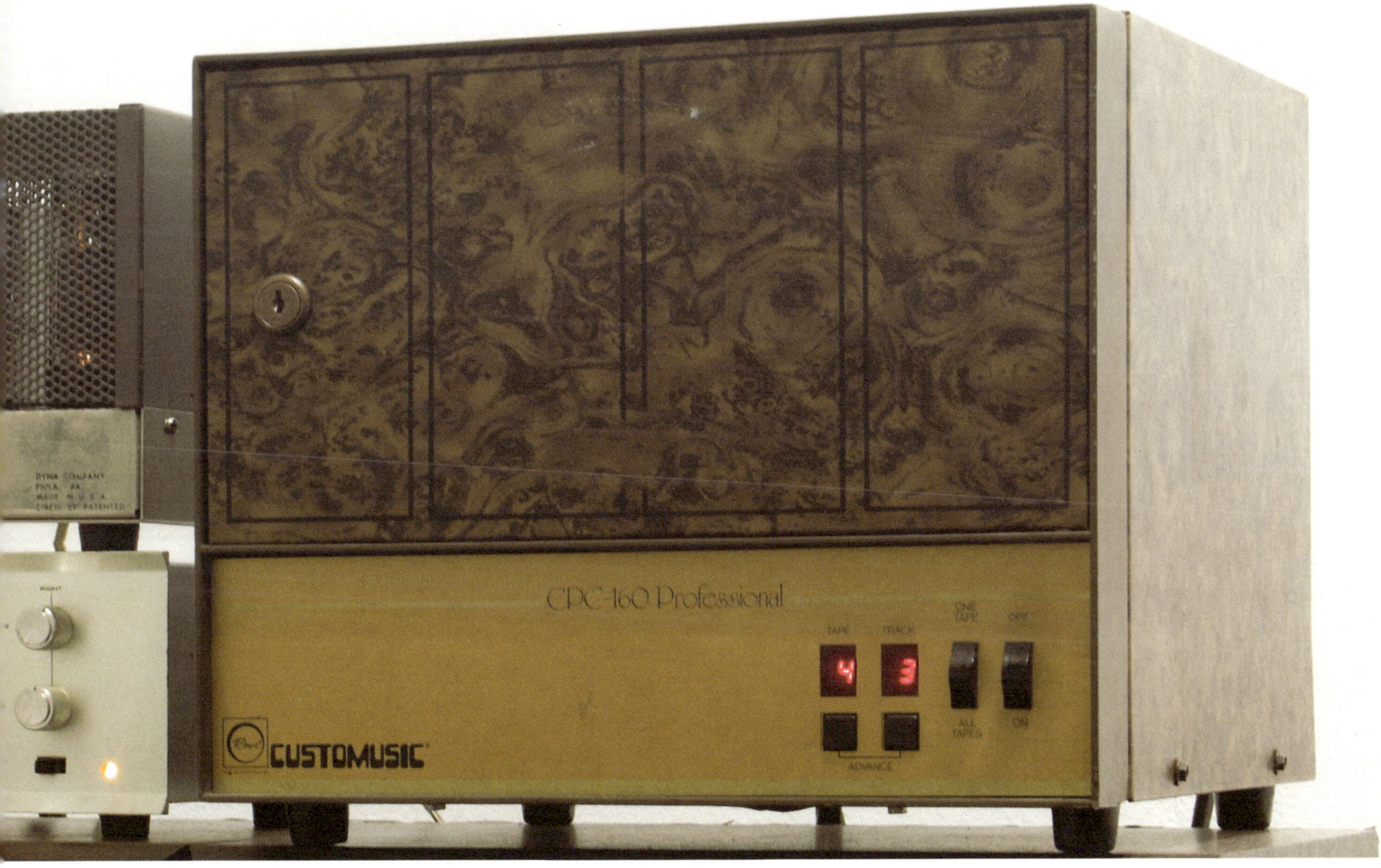
CPC-160 Professional
TAPE
TRACK
ONE TAPE
OFF
ALL TAPES
ON
ADVANCE
CUSTOMUSIC

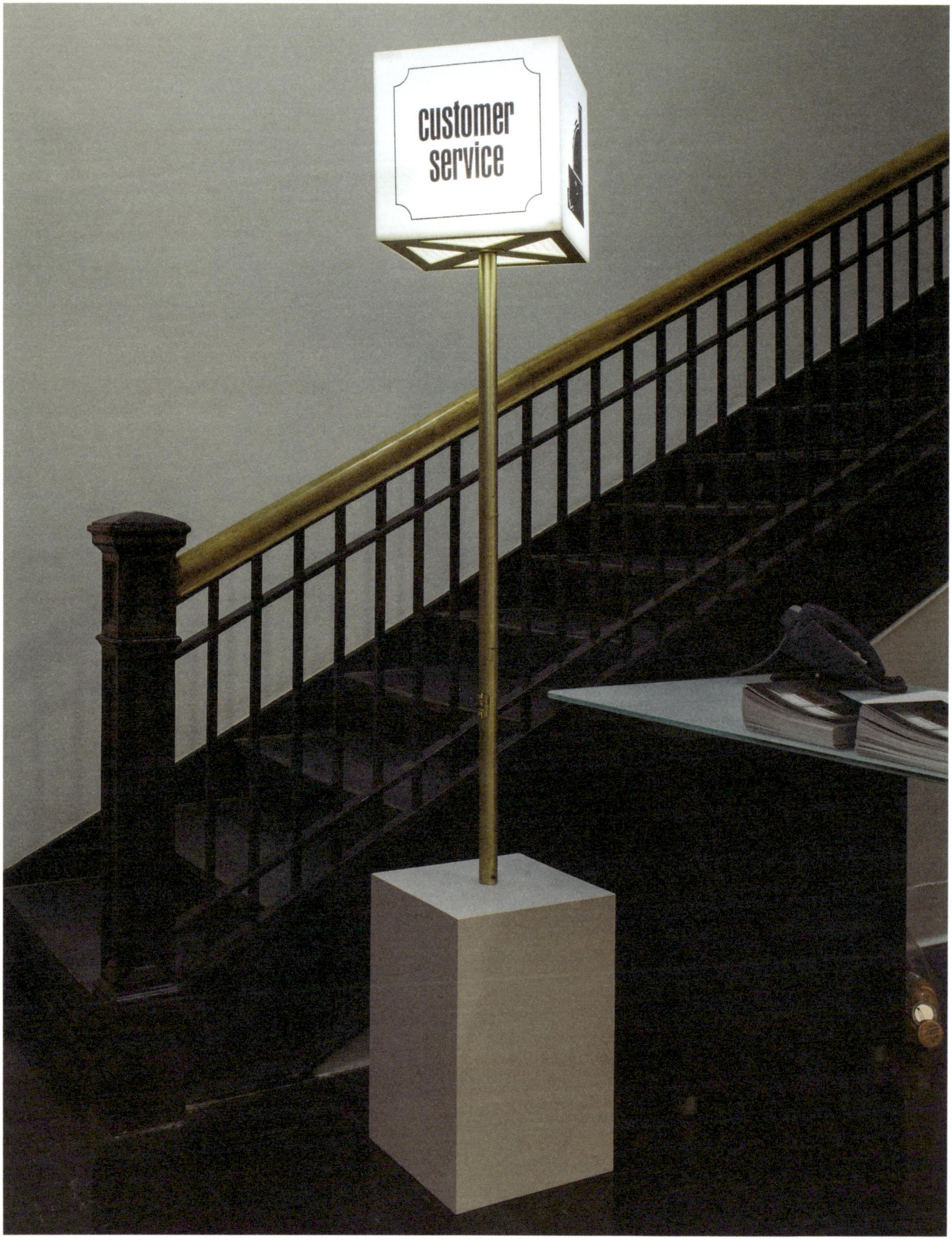
customer
service

You are cordially invited to attend

a Preview Cocktail Party celebrating

the Presentation Opening of

Dixie Square Mall

15201 Dixie Highway, Harvey, Illinois

August 23, 1966

from 7 o'clock P.M. to 9 o'clock P.M.

Please present this
Invitation at the
Montgomery Ward
Mall Court

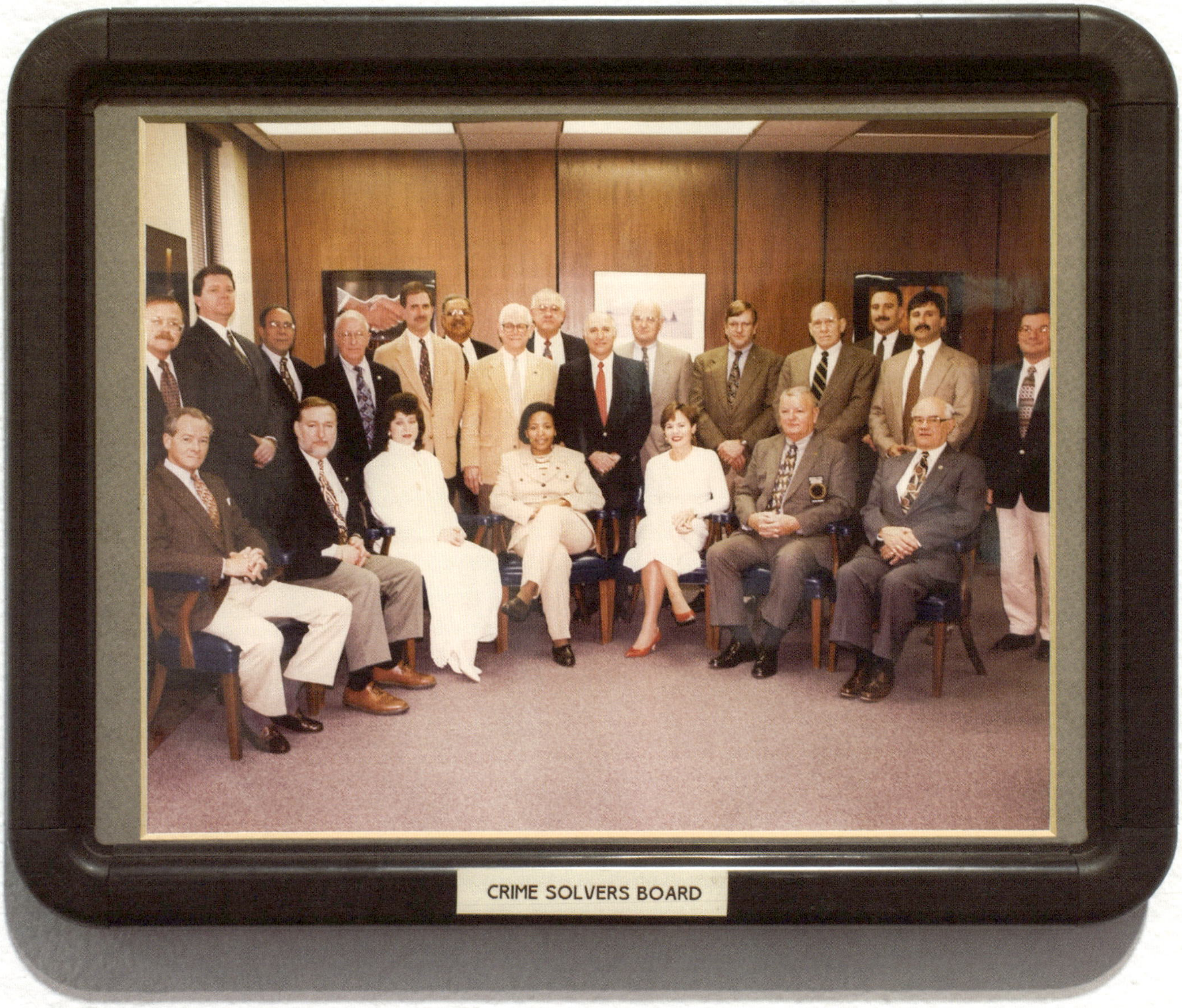
CRIME SOLVERS BOARD

CLOSE OUT
Exhibition Checklist

Dimensions are given in inches, by height × width × depth. All works are lent courtesy of the artist.

1. *What You Reinforce Is What You Get*, 2013
Installation of found paper ephemera and photographs
Overall dimensions variable

2. *A Thief Has a Hard Time*, 2012
Installation of found Polaroids
Each of 96 photographs, 4¼ × 3½; overall dimensions variable

3. *The Great Prosperity*, 2012
Installation of 24 prints made from found negatives
Each of 3 prints, 44 × 54; each of 21 prints, 13 × 16; overall dimensions variable

4. *Plat of Survey, Dixie Square Mall*, 2012
Ink on paper
36 × 41½

5. *JC Penney Court, Rolling Acres Mall*, 2012
Inkjet print made from found ink-and-watercolor drawing
40 × 50

6. *Dixie Square Mall Center Court*, 2012
Inkjet print made from found architect's rendering
40 × 50

7. *Rowe Customusic CPC-160 Professional*, 2012
Tape player with cassettes, amplifier, and speakers
11¾ × 13½ × 13½, player only

8. *Montgomery Ward Door Pulls*, 2011
Installation of found milled-aluminum handles
Each of 10 elements, 9 × 6; overall 9 × 78

9. *Customer Service*, 2011
Electric retail sign
54 × 12 × 12

10. *Crime Solvers Board*, 2011
Framed color photograph
9½ × 12 × 1

11. *Winner*, 2011
Polaroid
4¼ × 3½

12. *Price Labels, Jewel Food Store, Dixie Square Mall*, 2009–12
Silkscreen on paper
Each of 6 framed works, 19 × 13

13. *Art for Less #5*, 2009–11
Electric retail sign
24½ × 204½ × 5½

14. *Toys and Gifts*, 2009–10
Electric retail sign
68 × 94 × 9½

15. *Preview Invitation, Dixie Square Mall*, 2009
Ink on paper
7⅞ × 4⅞

BRIAN ULRICH, born in 1971 in Northport, New York, has exhibited his photographs extensively since receiving his MFA from Columbia College, Chicago, in 2004, including solo exhibitions at the Cleveland Museum of Art; Museum of Contemporary Art, Chicago; Nerman Museum of Contemporary Art, Overland Park, Kansas; Museum of Contemporary Art, San Diego; Rhona Hoffman Gallery, Chicago; Julie Saul Gallery, New York; and Robert Koch Gallery, San Francisco. In 2009, he received a John Simon Guggenheim Memorial Fellowship. In 2011, in conjunction with the Cleveland Museum of Art, Aperture published his first monograph, *Is This Place Great or What*. Ulrich currently lives in Richmond, where he is Assistant Professor in the Department of Photography and Film at the VCU School of the Arts.

Published in conjunction with the exhibition *Close Out: Retail Relics and Ephemera* (January 18–March 10, 2013), organized by the Anderson Gallery and made possible with generous support from the Office of the Dean, VCU School of the Arts.

Editor
Ashley Kistler

Book Design
Common Name
New York, NY

Printing
James River Press
Richmond, VA

Library of Congress Control Number
2012955695
ISBN 978-0-935519-01-3

Anderson Gallery
School of the Arts
Virginia Commonwealth University
907½ West Franklin Street
P.O. Box 842514
Richmond, VA 23284
804–828–1522
www.arts.vcu.edu/andersongallery

With special thanks to:
Joe Seipel
Ashley Kistler
Michael Lease
Traci Garland
Mark Waldhauser
Ken Meier
Yoonjai Choi
Will Steacy
Fred & Laura Bidwell
Paul Thulin
Shane Rocheleau
Tim Smith
Susan Worsham
Stanley Wolukau-Wanambwa
Claire Demos
Charles Freger
Justin James Reed
Kevin Murphy
Charles Monaghan
Greg Ruffing
Jon Gitelson
The Piece of Cake Collective
Rachelle Friesen
Aralie Caden Ulrich
Ryland Henrik Ulrich